A LABOR OF GRACE

A Labor of Grace

Saying Yes to God's Design for Pregnancy, Birth, and Motherhood

Madeline Marlatt

Published by Game Changer Publishing

Paperback ISBN: 979-8-90158-400-2

Hardcover ISBN: 979-8-90158-027-1

Digital ISBN: 979-8-90158-028-8

www.GameChangerPublishing.com

To Landen, Lily, Layla, and all my future children.
You led me to Jesus, and for that I am forever grateful.
I love you.

READ THIS FIRST

Just to say thank you for buying my book, I would like to connect!

Scan the QR Code Here:

A LABOR OF GRACE

Saying Yes to God's Design for Pregnancy, Birth, and Motherhood

MADELINE MARLATT

FOREWORD
BY EVAN MARLATT

"Let your guard down." A deep, booming voice that only I could hear. I had no question about what I had heard or who the voice came from. It is said that a child immediately recognizes the voice of their *Father*.

A couple of months before, Madeline and I had started a pursuit of God: reading the Bible, replacing secular music with worship music, praying, and seeking healing that we had not found from worldly means. Up to that point, Madeline and I believed in God, believed in Jesus, but really didn't know how that related to our lives.

A month after I heard this voice, my family was in town, and Madeline went to take a phone call upstairs. She was talking to our one Christian friend. That phone call led to her healing, deliverance, and her understanding that Jesus is alive! When I went upstairs, she told me what happened with tears in her eyes, and in that moment, I knew—the spirit of Truth descended upon me and removed the scales from my eyes. I didn't tell her she was crazy or imagining things. I just *knew*: Jesus is alive. The devil is real, but defeated. There is a spiritual war, but the victor is already decided.

I had truly *let my guard down* and *let God in*.

I had no idea how great a blessing it would be to get saved at the same time as my wife. We consumed testimonies of others coming to Jesus, and our whole experience began to make sense. Our faith was set on fire. God gave His only begotten Son, Jesus, so that we may have a personal relationship with God. If this only started after life, that would mean that death is our savior. Through the Holy Spirit, we can connect with Him directly! (John 14:26)

We immediately began to see God's hand in every challenge and triumph of our lives: past, present, and future. Together we experienced healing and freedom; purpose and clarity; refinement and growth.

This all happened after our first son was born, and we were focused on building a family. We saw God's grace in our son's birth, but we were surrounded by friends struggling with conceiving, miscarriages, pregnancy complications, and traumatic birth experiences, all causing fears and doubts in our own family. But we knew that there was more than meets the eye, and God helped us to see the schemes of the enemy to steal, kill, and destroy (John 10:10).

I have had the honor of seeing Madeline become an incredible woman of God, applying the Word of God to pregnancy, birth, postpartum, motherhood, and our marriage. She truly practices what she preaches. She pursues excellence in all that she does. She makes everyone around her better, especially me and our children.

Madeline has been blessed with an expectancy that God will move. We see His promises written throughout the Bible, and Madeline's faith has led to her seeing incredible answered prayers. Her heart is for your faith to increase as well!

God has placed an anointing on her life to help other women, but this book isn't only for moms. This book will help you improve your personal relationship with God—something made possible by the precious blood of Jesus Christ. This book will challenge you to become more aware and more disciplined, full of peace, joy, and goodness as fruit of the Holy Spirit. (Galatians 5:22-23)

I believe that this book will bless you and your family. It only takes one person to break the cycle in a family, and I believe that person is you. May the hand of God be on your life, your family, your health, your relationships, your finances, your heart, and your womb.

Father God, I pray that every reader begin to experience your overwhelming love in their life. I speak peace and comfort over every mother and father in Jesus' name. Holy Spirit, bring supernatural revelation to each and every reader. I pray that they hear your voice clearly. In Jesus' name, I pray. Amen!

CONTENTS

INTRODUCTION

I remember sitting on my couch, facing a difficult decision about how I was going to move forward in my third pregnancy. Would I choose faith or control?

My mind began to swirl back to a moment when I was pregnant with my first child. I distinctly remember hearing, *"I want the glory back."* I realized that much of my pregnancy and childbirth had been taken out of God's hands, or at least I had attempted to take it out of His hands. I didn't want to control everything during my pregnancy; I wanted to trust Him.

I understood that this experience was all for Him and that, no matter what happened, He deserved glory for every part of the process of bringing a child into this world. I knew that God would work everything for my good. Perhaps I was just going through a trial or facing a test, but I recognized it as a holy invitation from the Lord to surrender.

This holy invitation is God's call to surrender, to be refined during pregnancy and childbirth, and to carry this forward into motherhood. It is about becoming the version of yourself that God has called you to be and enjoying motherhood as a blessing rather than a burden. Accepting God's invitation to surrender and following Him during pregnancy and childbirth lays the foundation for a spirit-led, Christ-centered motherhood, and it is an invitation that the world cannot offer.

But there's more. Jesus didn't just die for you so you could have a ticket to heaven. Jesus didn't preach only salvation; He preached the Gospel of the Kingdom. His death and resurrection made that Kingdom accessible, but His message throughout His ministry was about the rule and reign of God breaking into the earth now.

Before I go any further, I want to show what Jesus *did* preach. Matthew 4:23 (NLT) says, *"Jesus traveled throughout the region of Galilee, teaching in the synagogues and announcing the Good News about the Kingdom. And he healed every kind of disease and illness."* Jesus didn't just preach forgiveness of sins; He demonstrated the Kingdom's power through healing and restoration; heaven touching earth.

Matthew 9:35 (NLT) adds, *"Jesus traveled through all the towns and villages of that area, teaching in the synagogues and announcing the Good News about the Kingdom. And he healed every kind of disease and illness."* This repeats His mission: not only salvation, but the Kingdom's reign manifesting in everyday life. And lastly, the Lord's Prayer in Matthew 6:10 reveals Jesus's heart: salvation brings us into the Kingdom, but the goal is to see God's rule expressed on earth in all areas of our lives.

God's holy invitation is about living under the full gospel of the Kingdom, saying yes to God's Kingdom plans instead of just "being saved and surviving." If we stop at the gospel of salvation, we'll live as lukewarm Christians and moms: saved but powerless, feeling constantly anxious and overwhelmed, stuck in survival mode, and believing that pregnancy is a burden and just something you endure, and motherhood is draining instead of life-giving.

But when you step into the gospel of the Kingdom, when you accept God's invitation, you can step into peace instead of fear, knowing that He reigns over every aspect of our lives: pregnancy, birth, and beyond into our homes, children, and emotions. You receive authority instead of defeat, going through these seasons not in your own strength, but in His power. And you access purpose instead of mundanity, seeing it all (diapers, dishes, discipline, pregnancy, and birth) as Kingdom assignments.

I didn't write this book because I have all the answers about pregnancy, childbirth, or even motherhood. I am still surrendering, learning, and growing every day. I wrote this book because accepting God's invitation to surrender, to be refined and sanctified during my own journeys of pregnancy, childbirth, and motherhood, has been the best decision I could have ever made. I am learning what it means to follow God's design in all things, and motherhood doesn't feel like a burden. It feels like walking in His presence and power daily. I want you to know that you can encounter God during this time, too.

Writing this book felt like more than just a project; it was an act of obedience and a calling to help women awaken to the sacredness of this season. During my first pregnancy, I knew of Jesus, but I didn't truly know Him. I didn't have a strong relationship with Him. However, as soon as I became pregnant, I felt a shift within myself and developed a desire to seek Him.

I believe God was pursuing me during this time. I distinctly remember the moment when I first felt His presence. I was on a walk in my neighborhood in Austin, Texas, which was under construction, with large, open grassy lots. While walking, I put on worship music, something I had actually never done before. The first song that played was "The Blessing" by Kari Jobe.

As I came across a long, expansive meadow, I began to cry. I was confused and didn't realize that I was feeling the presence of God at that moment, but I knew it was significant and tied to Him. I believe that was the moment I first sensed God's presence, sparking something within me and igniting a desire to draw closer to Him. It's a bit hard to explain that moment.

After that, I started listening to worship music and occasionally looking at scripture, inviting God into the process of pregnancy and birth. I prayed and asked Him for what I needed, and I had immense faith.

However, what I was missing during my pursuit of God was surrender. I believed in Jesus at the time and felt like I loved Him, but He wasn't yet my Lord. I still was trying to control much of my life rather than doing it God's way.

When the time came for the birth of my first child, I was blown away by the experience. For the first time, I knew not only that God had to be real, but that He cared about my baby and me and would answer my prayers if I prayed them. This experience intensified my desire to know God better, but at the time, I really didn't know how.

Life continued as usual. I thoroughly enjoyed becoming a new mom and watching my son grow and hit milestones. However, despite having such a positive experience entering motherhood, I still suffered from immense anxiety. Because I loved being a mom so much, my desire to have another child grew strong very quickly after my son's birth, but for some reason, I felt incredibly nervous about having another baby.

Fears surrounding secondary infertility, whether and when we would be able to have another baby, began to creep in unexpectedly. Despite having no history of infertility, I found myself consumed by worry. It was during this time that the desire for control took hold of me. I started obsessing over my health, doing everything possible to ensure there would be no obstacles to having another child.

This anxiety robbed me of so much joy during this season. When my son was ten months old, my worries about having another baby reached their peak. One evening, while working out in my basement, I stumbled upon a video about the demonic roots of yoga.

To give you some context, I had been on a self-help and health journey for the ten years leading up to this point. I practiced yoga religiously, initially to address various aches and pains, and found it genuinely beneficial. This led me to explore other healing modalities that also provided some great results, but I never felt truly "healed."

However, after watching that video, I felt something was off. At the time, I didn't have many Christian friends, except for one girl I knew who loved Jesus and often spoke about Him. The day after watching the video, I reached out to her and shared my experience and how it had made me feel unsettled. This eventually led to a deep conversation about Jesus, during which she suggested that I might need deliverance and that He could help me.

That was the catalyst for a profound encounter with the Holy Spirit, which took place in my bathroom. In an instant, everything changed. If you've read or heard people describe their encounters with Jesus or being born again, my experience was exactly that. It was as if the veil had been lifted from my eyes; I could finally see the truth, recognize the lies I had believed for so long, and understand the control I had exerted in my life in pursuit of health.

In the moment of truly meeting Jesus, I realized He had been with me all along, and I became a new person. Suddenly, all those anxieties and worries about my health and the possibility of having another baby vanished. I came to understand that God had been in control the entire time and that, when it was meant for us to have another child, it would happen.

A couple of months later, I conceived our second child, and from the very start of that pregnancy, everything felt different. I knew I could pray to God, trusting that He would be with me. What truly set this experience apart was the sense of surrender in my heart. I no longer felt the need to control the outcome; I understood that my actions alone wouldn't determine the success of my pregnancy and birth.

My outlook changed from one of control to one of faith. It felt like a huge burden had been lifted off my shoulders. I no longer felt the pressure to perform and do everything perfectly. As God says, "*His yoke is easy, and His burden is light*" (Matthew 11:28 KJV), and that is precisely how I felt during my second pregnancy.

There were many moments throughout this pregnancy when I noticed the peace I had, in stark contrast to the anxiety I once experienced. For instance, when I went for my twenty-week anatomy scan with my first child, I was filled with fear and anxiety, desperate to know if there were any issues. In contrast, during my second pregnancy, I approached the scan with a sense of peace, fully aware that the outcome was not in my control.

By the end of my second pregnancy, I could clearly see a complete shift in how I felt and how I reacted to various situations.

The first time I was pregnant, I felt an overwhelming urge to do everything I could to ensure my baby was born successfully in the way I desired. I wanted to control every aspect of the situation, just like I had heard others doing. However, during my second pregnancy, I experienced a sense of peace, trusting that God was in control and that my baby would be born at the perfect time. I realized that the smoothness of my first birth was not solely due to my efforts but also to God's wisdom guiding my preparation and His grace surrounding me.

I should mention that after having my first baby, I became a doula because I wanted to gain professional experience to help other women through childbirth. But it wasn't until after my encounter with Jesus and during my second pregnancy that I felt a strong prompting to share my journey and the lessons I had learned from both pregnancies.

I decided to share tips and insights about childbirth and my journey of following Jesus on an Instagram page, which I named *Momma Madeline*. This platform evolved into more than just documenting my life and pregnancy.

After committing my life to Jesus, I noticed a significant shift in how I approached conceiving a child and experiencing pregnancy. I felt compelled to share my transformation, believing that the strong nudge to create an Instagram account was from God. As I remained obedient and continued to share my experiences, my following grew.

The content I shared on Instagram became the foundation and passion for this book. I invite Christian women to walk through pregnancy, birth, and motherhood with Jesus. My goal is to help you accept the Lord's holy invitation to build trust in God, not just in your own strength. This journey will encourage you to train your heart to hear His voice more clearly, shift your identity from an "I must do it all" mindset to "He's with me," prepare for the spiritual warfare that comes with motherhood, and sanctify your view of being a mother. I learned that I couldn't do it alone, and I needed to accept God's invitation in this season.

The Holy Spirit is our helper, counselor, comforter, advocate, teacher, and guide into all truth (John 14:26; John 16:13). Isn't this exactly what every expecting mother needs on her journey into motherhood? My intention is to provide you with encouragement, practical tools, and biblical truths to help you navigate a culture filled with fear and performance.

This book isn't a soft, fluffy, feel-good pregnancy devotional; it's a call to surrender, to confront and dismantle modern idols like control, fear, self-reliance, and medical dependency, which can hinder women from walking in the freedom and power God intended. There is a cultural misconception that pregnancy is merely a physical process, but I invite you to see it as a holy refining fire, a season of spiritual formation, and preparation for motherhood in God's Kingdom.

By the end of this book, I hope you will have dismantled idols and replaced them with truth, feel confident in walking with discernment and partnering with the Holy Spirit, perceive pregnancy and birth as a beautiful, sacred process designed by God rather than just a medical event, and experience a shift in your perspective of motherhood. I want you to step into spirit-led motherhood with peace, purpose, and boldness, fully accepting the Lord's holy invitation to partner with Him through pregnancy, childbirth, and motherhood, seeing these seasons as sacred Kingdom assignments rather than just physical experiences.

PART 1

THE CALL TO SURRENDER

Lord, I open my heart to Your holy invitation. Refine me, search me, and remove anything within me that is not from You. I don't want to rely on the world while navigating pregnancy and motherhood. I want to walk by Your Spirit. Teach me Your ways, reveal Your design, and prepare me for the kind of motherhood that brings You glory. I say yes to Your presence, Your wisdom, Your plan, Your power, and Your call to surrender.

In Jesus's name, amen.

1

THE SACRED INVITATION

Before I became pregnant with my first child, I felt a deep desire for a natural pregnancy and birth. I believed that I was designed to experience this and that medical intervention wasn't a necessity unless there was a valid reason to consider otherwise. As someone who aspired to have a natural, holistic pregnancy and birth, I was attracted to the "crunchy" home-birth community. In this community, I observed a strong emphasis on reclaiming birth for women and regaining our power.

As women, we are the authority, fully in control. Birth is sovereign and sacred. Many acknowledge pregnancy and childbirth as sacred, yet I believe that some have either forgotten or never understood what this truly means.

"Sacred" doesn't equate to aligning with feminine energy or awakening your inner goddess. "Sacred" means holy and set apart. It signifies that this moment, this season, belongs to God. Birth is not a pathway to your higher self; rather, it's a divine invitation to meet the Most High God.

Giving birth isn't the place to reclaim your power; it's where you lay it down and discover that His strength is made perfect in your weakness. You don't need to be a goddess; you need the presence of God. You don't need to ascend; you need to surrender.

This process is sacred, not because of your power, but because of His presence. Birth is sacred, not due to your co-creation of life with the universe, but because of the holy God who created it. The world promotes an illusion of control during pregnancy, placing us women in the driver's seat and, conversely, elevating medical systems and teams to the role of savior.

From my own experiences during pregnancy, I've realized there are two choices: self-reliance or surrender. Pregnancy often has a way of dismantling the illusion of self-sufficiency, and if you allow it, it will lead you to the feet of Jesus.

Pregnancy reminds us that we not only need practical help but also saving grace. We require a Redeemer who sees, sustains, strengthens, and saves us. Pregnancy frequently brings physical exhaustion, emotional ups and downs, and mental overwhelm. You soon realize you can't control everything: your body, your baby's development, or the future. This marks the beginning of the call to surrender, your holy invitation.

PREGNANCY AS A SACRED PARTNERSHIP WITH GOD

So, how is pregnancy a call to intimacy with God? It is an invitation to co-labor with Him. It's an opportunity to recognize that you are not alone and that you get to partner with the Creator of life. Pregnancy often slows you down, alters your routines, and amplifies your awareness of your limitations.

All of this creates space to lean into the Lord. It takes you out of the power seat and places Him in it. It is also an invitation to depend on God more fully.

Pregnancy can bring moments of fear and worry, but every anxious thought that arises is an opportunity to surrender and lean on God's strength. It creates the space to pray without ceasing, turning every worry, negative thought, or anxious moment into a prayer. It's an invitation to hear His voice more clearly.

Pregnancy is a time to attune ourselves, to listen in stillness, to seek God, and to speak with Him. Many women often say that their dreams become more vivid and intense while pregnant, which I believe happens because their bodies are more spiritually sensitive during this time. God frequently communicates with us through dreams, scripture, quietude, and stirring emotions.

This experience invites us to trust in His design. Pregnancy is humbling; it reveals that we are not in control. During my first pregnancy, it became very clear to me that there was a profound purpose behind the entire process of pregnancy and birth.

Realizing that I had no control over what was happening in my body prompted me to learn more about God's design and the divine process. It encourages us to worship while we wait. Pregnancy teaches us patience, as it is an active season of anticipation.

This divine design fosters peace through worship in the waiting. It offers an invitation to experience God's heart as a parent. Through pregnancy, we begin to comprehend God's protective love, gentleness, and willingness to sacrifice for His children.

It's no coincidence that God describes Himself as a Father and even as one who gives birth to new things (Isaiah 42:14; 66:9). Pregnancy provides a glimpse of the love God has for us, contrasting the world's expectations with what God invites us to embrace. Before I delve into the comparisons, I want to acknowledge that I felt and experienced each of these contrasts during my pregnancy.

When considering what the world offers versus what I experienced from God, here's what I found:

- Fear: The world presents fear of miscarriage, pain, and uncertain outcomes, while God offers a peace that surpasses all understanding (Philippians 4:7).
- Control: The world promotes control through checklists,

plans, and protocols, while God invites us to surrender to His purpose (Jeremiah 29:11).

- Self-Reliance: The world encourages a mindset of *You've got this*, whereas God calls us to depend on His Spirit and trust that He has us in His care (Romans 8:28).
- Perfection: The world values the perfect body image, an ideal birth story, and a flawless nursery, while God extends grace for all the messy moments of pregnancy and beyond (2 Corinthians 12:9).
- Noise: The world inundates us with opinions, apps, and information overload, but God offers stillness and discernment of His presence (Psalm 46:10).
- Medical Management: The world often defaults to medical management, while God provides His divine design as the starting point of pregnancy (John 1:3).
- Validation: The world seeks validation from others, but God roots our identity in Christ as His beloved daughters (1 Peter 2:9).
- Comfort: The world prioritizes comfort at all costs, whereas God offers us refinement through the process for His glory (Isaiah 48:10).
- Anxiety: The world breeds anxiety about almost every outcome, while God invites us to have faith in His promises (Matthew 11:28).

CHOOSING WHICH PATH TO FOLLOW

So, how do we choose God's invitation over the world's?

We need to recognize that the world is constantly communicating through various channels, including culture, social media, doctors, and even well-meaning friends. So, we need to slow down and create space for God. We should consistently pray, seek the Holy Spirit for discernment, and choose to surrender each day. Walking by faith daily and surrounding ourselves with people who speak the truth is crucial, and we must continue to say yes, even when it's difficult.

I want to share an example of how I fell into the world's invitation for pregnancy during my first experience. As I prepared for my first baby's arrival, I focused on various aspects: physical, mental, and spiritual. I prayed and asked God for very specific things. At that time, my relationship with Jesus was not as strong as it is now, so my prayers felt more like, "God, I believe you can do this for me; I believe you love me, but will you do this for me?" I often asked, "Will you make these things happen for me?"

Everything was new to me. At that time, I wasn't a born-again believer. I believed in Jesus, but I wasn't actively seeking Him as my Lord or surrendering to Him. Although I was inviting Him into the process, I experienced significant inner conflict. I had friends who were also becoming first-time moms, and they were following the traditional medical route for childbirth, adhering to the common worldview of birth.

I remember talking to them about their experiences, including all their appointments and various ultrasounds. I already had a strong desire to pursue a more natural approach to childbirth. I understood the difference between an OB-GYN's approach to birth and a midwife's, so I knew I wanted to choose the midwife route. However, this meant I would have fewer ultrasounds and fewer check-ins during my pregnancy compared to my friends, which stressed me out.

My concerns prompted me to seek out a private ultrasound at a separate facility because I felt the need to see my baby and ensure everything was okay, as if I had some control over the situation.

Before reaching the twenty-week mark with my first child, I saw four different providers before finally settling on one. I ended up switching to a homebirth midwife around twenty-two weeks. At that point, I decided to let go of any comparisons to what everyone else was doing. I had a strong conviction that God was showing me a different way to approach my pregnancy. None of my friends or acquaintances were considering home births, but I felt strongly that it was the right choice for me.

Once I made the switch to a homebirth midwife, I found a sense of peace and focused entirely on what I felt called to do, rather than worrying about others' paths. I am not saying homebirth is always "following God's path" or accepting His invitation, but in my situation, I felt it was.

After I became a born-again believer and fully surrendered my life to Jesus, I entered my second pregnancy with a new perspective. As a doula, I understood the importance of having a birth plan and being well-prepared. However, I came to realize that no matter how perfect my plan was, it meant very little if I wasn't praying and speaking God's word into my situation more than I was preparing.

So, in my second pregnancy, I recognized the crucial contrast: while having a plan is essential, it's even more important to be praying, aligning my words and actions with His word, and surrendering our plans to Him. This opened my eyes to the idols in my heart and what was actually stopping me from surrendering in the first place. In the next chapter, we will dive deeper into this.

QUESTIONS FOR REFLECTION

1. When I think about being pregnant and growing new life, do I immediately turn to God in gratitude or to the world for answers?
2. What lies or fears has the world planted in me about pregnancy, and what does God's Word say instead?
3. How might this season of pregnancy be an invitation to deepen my dependence on Jesus rather than my own understanding?
4. What would it look like for me to embrace pregnancy as

part of God's purpose, not something to manage, but something to partner with Him in?

5. What is one step I can take today to say "yes" to God, even if it looks different from what the world expects?

2

RECOGNIZING MODERN IDOLS

A significant part of accepting and choosing God's invitation is putting Him first. However, how can we prioritize Him when we place other things before Him?

I have come to terms with many things I have put before God. He has highlighted them to me over time, and I invite you, in this moment, to ask the Holy Spirit to highlight what you have or are putting before Him.

Here are some examples for myself: fear, health, expectations for a perfect birth, specific outcomes like a home birth, an ideal pregnancy, timelines, expert opinions, information, comfort, pain-free births, and self-sufficiency.

WHEN PEACE BECOMES PERFORMANCE

During my first pregnancy, I mentioned I was drawn to the crunchy homebirth community. There is a lot of beauty in that space, such as honoring the natural design of our bodies, making informed choices, and believing that birth does not have to be feared. However, there is also a heavy emphasis on taking back your power in childbirth, suggesting that you can control birth with the right mindset and find peace through techniques like hypnobirthing. This often involves entering a self-induced hypnotic state or clearing your mind through relaxation scripts and visualizations.

Although I didn't delve deeply into some of the more new-age practices associated with home birth, a topic for another day, I found myself caught up in this mindset. I believed that, while I trusted God, I was in control through my efforts, which created a lot of pressure.

I remember thinking, *if anything goes wrong, people will blame me.* This mindset was rooted in the world's perspective of our own control rather than in the truth that God is sovereign over all things, but often waits for agreement, prayer, or declaration before moving, including in our births. As a first-time mom, I eagerly anticipated meeting my baby, but I succumbed to the societal notion that we control when our babies are born, even believing it was acceptable to pick their birthday.

Toward the end of my pregnancy, my patience wore thin. I wanted to take matters into my own hands, trying all the methods others recommended to induce labor: curb walking, dancing, long walks, acupuncture, and spicy food. This left me feeling stressed, burnt out, confused, and frustrated. Ultimately, it was nothing I did that brought my baby into the world; he arrived when he was ready.

During my second pregnancy, new idols emerged, threatening my surrender to God. While I let go of the need to control my pregnancy and birth this time, I soon realized I was idolizing a "perfect experience."

I became preoccupied with how quickly my second labor would progress, especially since my first labor had been fairly quick at eight hours. I worried about whether my birth photographer would make it in time. If she didn't arrive, how would I capture and share this beautiful experience with people? What if I had no photos? God quickly reminded me that I was focusing more on everything going exactly as I wanted than on how He intended it to be. These concerns may seem trivial, but handing them over to God transformed my relationship with Him.

During my third pregnancy, I thought I would be free of these idols, but I was quickly reminded that each pregnancy is unique, with its own set of fears, anxieties, and distractions that can hinder true surrender and the peace that comes with it.

The two biggest idols I faced during my third pregnancy were fear and information. It all began when I received blood work results indicating that my progesterone levels were on the lower end of the spectrum. Upon receiving this information, I allowed fear to creep in and dominate my thought process. Anxiety took hold, and I realized that I was prioritizing fear over my faith in God. However, after spending time in prayer, God redirected me to the truth. Ultimately, I was able to make decisions based on peace instead of fear.

The hardest idol to confront throughout all my pregnancies has undoubtedly been the desire for control. I believe this is one of the main struggles women face during pregnancy, as the need for control often arises in response to fear, fear of suffering, disappointment, pain, or loss.

Our desire to protect ourselves often leads us to distrust the protective hand of our Father. Wanting to control outcomes reveals the lie that we believe we are in charge. However, control is often just a false sense of security. If we truly believed that God is good, faithful, wise, and sovereign, and that His word is true, why would we feel the need to take control?

WHEN IDOLS SPEAK LOUDER THAN GOD

We tend to grip tighter when we doubt that His way is better than ours. So, it is important to address and dismantle our idols, as they distract us from hearing God's voice.

When we focus on fear, control, or outcomes, we stop listening for His guidance. Our minds become cluttered with noise, leaving little room for stillness with Him. As a result, we may make harmful decisions instead of wise ones.

Idols replace God as our source of peace. Instead of turning to Him, we seek peace in birth plans, doctors, affirmation, or research. Yet, when these things change or fail us, our peace is shaken because it was built on sand, not on the solid rock of faith.

Idols can also block our intimacy with God. He desires our whole hearts, and when we withhold certain areas, like fears, timelines, or a craving for control, we have not fully surrendered. This creates distance, not because God leaves us, but because we are keeping Him at arm's length.

Moreover, idols breed exhaustion and anxiety. The effort to maintain control, perfection, or comfort can be draining. It burdens us, while Jesus invites us to find rest in Him.

Lastly, idols rob God of His glory. When we attribute our peace, outcomes, or strengths to anything other than Him, we are stealing glory that rightfully belongs to God. Surrendering our idols brings us back to worship, reminding us that every good thing comes from Him.

WHOSE REPORT SHOULD I BELIEVE?

Each pregnancy has been challenging for me in different ways in terms of prioritizing God's Word over expert opinions, like those of my midwife. For example, when I was informed about having low progesterone during my third pregnancy, it was difficult to maintain my trust in God.

It's easy to say we believe in Him, but when a doctor or midwife, someone considered an expert, gives us information, it's hard not to accept it without question. Our society has ingrained the idea that these professionals are the ultimate authorities, especially in areas such as pregnancy and birth, where they are often portrayed as saviors. I get it!

You hear stories frequently in which individuals, after having a baby, recount their experiences and often glorify their providers. It's not that doctors and midwives are bad; rather, society has placed them on a pedestal, and I have faced this personally as well.

The initial reaction for me when I receive any information from a provider is to want to believe them, but then it goes directly to trying to control the situation and the outcomes. When I learned that my progesterone levels were low, my initial reaction was to do everything I could to increase them.

There was a time when I felt an overwhelming sense of anxiety, especially related to my fear of losing a baby. I felt immense pressure, believing that if I didn't do everything right, I could face a terrible loss.

I started researching natural ways to boost progesterone. I looked into what I could eat, how much sleep I needed, and whether I should consider medication or natural progesterone. My instinct was to control the situation as much as possible.

During that time, I had a tight lump in my throat, my heart raced, and I often felt sick to my stomach. Over several days, as I took the time to pray and spend quiet moments with the Lord, I began to surrender my worries to Him. This process wasn't instantaneous; it took patience and reflection.

I did take some sensible steps, as I learned about natural ways to increase progesterone, which I felt was wise and in line with what God was showing me. The major shift for me came in letting go of the need for control. I leaned on my faith, the Word of God, the authority God gave me to claim anything that is already mine from the shed blood of Jesus (like my health) and also reached out to friends who are believers to pray for me. I chose to pause my relentless research and instead focused on prayer and surrounding myself with supportive voices.

Eventually, I experienced a profound peace that surpassed all understanding. I felt a physical change in my body. The symptoms of anxiety began to fade away. My heart stopped racing, the lump in my throat disappeared, and I no longer felt that sense of dread. Instead, I started to feel hope again. This transformation reassured me that I was on the right path, one aligned with God's will.

We are conditioned to believe that if a doctor advises something, we should follow that guidance. This is where I believe God and His word play a crucial role. Just because an expert provides information, it doesn't necessarily mean it's the ultimate truth. Facts may not be truth; God's word is truth. Hear me when I say that not all information is bad and not all medical providers are bad. However, I've learned that everything needs to be taken to the Father.

I've even heard stories where women were told by their doctors that there was no heartbeat during an ultrasound. They would be informed that they were going to miscarry, but some of them, especially those who are believers, still held on to the faith that everything would be okay. Surprisingly, when they returned for another appointment, they found a healthy baby with a heartbeat.

These types of experiences happen quite frequently. I've heard numerous stories of doctors providing one diagnosis, only for it to turn out to be incorrect. I remind myself that while information from experts can sometimes be helpful, we need to exercise discernment. Ultimately, God is the true healer, and although He is sovereign over everything, He's also looking for believers willing to partner with the Word in faith and will move accordingly (James 4:2).

Those kinds of stories are really striking. I've heard more than just pregnancy-related ones. For example, doctors sometimes make claims that turn out to be untrue. I remember hearing about a woman who was diagnosed with cancer. The doctors told her she had only three months to live. Tragically, she died three months later, but after her autopsy, it was revealed that there was no cancer at all.

It's astounding that these kinds of things can happen. This has shown me that God is in control, but what we speak and agree with also matters (Proverbs 18:21). We need to use discernment and not elevate the opinions and expertise of doctors above God's Word and His truth. We need to be careful about what we speak over ourselves, our babies, and our circumstances, and what we allow to take root in our hearts and minds.

AWARENESS LEADS TO FREEDOM

Maybe you're reading this, and you're thinking, *Wow, I didn't even realize fear and control were idols for me. What can I do?* What I suggest is to examine your day-to-day actions and the motivations behind them. Personally, I didn't realize that I had idols in my life. I was unaware that my actions were creating a barrier between God and me. This behavior seems normal because so many people engage in it.

For instance, many people often talk about their anxiety or fear on social media, sharing what they googled during their first trimester. It has become so normalized to feel anxious and believe we can control situations through information.

Take a moment to reflect on your daily activities. Are you constantly searching for information on Google or ChatGPT? Are you asking questions that perhaps should be addressed through prayer and God's guidance? Sometimes, we think we're helping ourselves by gathering information, but for me, more information often leads to more fear and anxiety, which is not from God. Evaluate your activities and how they make you feel.

If your search brings you more stress than comfort, you're likely seeking answers in the wrong place. You might be looking for peace but not finding it through these channels.

The amazing news is there is hope in Jesus, and in later chapters, I will share how we can practically surrender to God during this challenging and inviting season of pregnancy.

QUESTIONS FOR REFLECTION

1. What do I rely on most for comfort or control besides God: my routines, information, or advice from others?
2. Have I been comparing my experience to others, and how has that taken my focus off trusting God's plan for me?
3. When I feel anxious about my body, my baby, or the birth, what am I trying to control instead of surrendering it to God?
4. How can I invite God into my daily moments so He is truly first?
5. Which habits, expectations, or worries have become idols in my heart, and how can I let God transform them?

3

IS THAT YOU, GOD?

Remember when I mentioned that one of the main struggles women face during pregnancy is a desire for a sense of control? This desire often stems from fear: fear of suffering, disappointment, pain, or loss.

I understand this from speaking with thousands of women and experiencing it myself. This response shows a desire to protect ourselves rather than to trust in the protective hand of our Father. It's not easy! In our efforts to avoid pain during pregnancy, we will inevitably encounter moments of uncertainty.

There may be unknowns, confusing information, and unexpected circumstances. How we respond to these challenges is crucial. We can choose either faith or fear.

Our reactions to difficult information or personal worries will depend on one key factor: where God fits into it all. Did we accept God's invitation? I assure you, He is always present, but we also need to invite Him into our decision-making process. God sent His Holy Spirit to be with us, act as our counselor, and guide us into all truth. There is no better time to seek His counsel and wisdom than during a season like this.

THE BATTLE FOR OUR SOULS

Before I continue, it's important to emphasize something else: pregnancy and birth are more than just physical experiences; they are deeply spiritual.

You must recognize that a spiritual war is being waged over your soul, your husband's soul, and, from the moment you conceive a child, for their soul as well. The moment sin entered the world through Adam and Eve's disobedience, this spiritual war began.

Satan, the enemy, seeks to "*steal, kill, and destroy*" (John 10:10 NIV). His goal is to separate us from God, instilling doubt about His goodness and fostering fear, shame, and self-reliance. Every day, we grapple with lies, temptation, fear, pride, and distractions that attempt to pull us away from full dependence on Jesus.

Pregnancy is a sacred season. As a woman, you become a vessel for new life, partnering with God in His act of creation. Because of this, the enemy fears godly motherhood and the legacy of faith that a woman can nurture both physically and spiritually. He targets women with fear, control, shame, and doubt to disrupt God's design for motherhood so we do not accept the full gospel of the Kingdom and walk in what is rightfully ours through the shed blood of Jesus.

Pregnancy amplifies our vulnerabilities but also our opportunities to depend on God. Just as Mary carried the Savior, women today carry promises that can change generations, making them targets for spiritual warfare.

Let me share a few examples of the spiritual warfare that I experienced during my pregnancy. I run an online ministry for women through social media, where I engage with hundreds of women about their pregnancies and births each week. The moment I found out I was pregnant, I started coming across an overwhelming number of posts about miscarriage. Women were messaging me about their losses, with many sharing their experiences of losing babies well into the second trimester or dealing with stillbirths.

While I know that this is part of the space I operate in, I couldn't help but wonder why it was happening at that moment. Was it just a coincidence? I don't see it that way.

One of the enemy's primary tactics is to attack our minds, planting seeds of doubt, fear, and anxiety. He communicates through thoughts that contradict God's Word, subtle suggestions that appeal to pride or fear, cultural messages and media that perpetuate lies masquerading as truth, and emotional spirals that cause us to forget God's promises. He can use comparison, shame, dreams, and the voices of others to create confusion.

Once I understood that we are engaged in a daily spiritual battle, it became clear to me that not everything I see, hear, or am told is from God, especially during pregnancy.

This spiritual battle runs deep. It's not just about you. It's about your baby and generations to come. Fear, anxiety, and stress can have negative impacts on unborn children, not just physically but also spiritually.

The evidence clearly shows that stress can physically impact a child in the womb.

- Elevated maternal stress is also linked with *shortened gestational age* (preterm births or earlier delivery) in some studies.[1]
- Elevated maternal cortisol during pregnancy is linked to changes in offspring hippocampus and amygdala volumes (important for stress regulation and emotion). For example, in one study, higher cortisol early in pregnancy was associated with a smaller hippocampus, altered amygdala volume, and increased risk of affective problems.[2]

---

1. "Sleep Deprivation Impairs the Suppression of Unwanted Thoughts and Memories," *Proceedings of the National Academy of Sciences of the United States of America* 116, no. 32 (2019), https://www.pnas.org/doi/full/10.1073/pnas.1905890116.

2. C. Buss, E. P. Davis, B. Shahbaba, J. C. Pruessner, K. Head, and C. A. Sandman, "Maternal cortisol over the course of pregnancy and subsequent child amygdala and hippocampus volumes and affective

- Prenatal stress predicts differences in infant cortisol reactivity to stressors. For example, infants whose mothers had more prenatal anxiety or stress show greater or altered cortisol responses at five weeks, eight weeks, five months, and twelve months in various stress paradigms.[3]
- There is a higher risk of internalizing disorders (anxiety, depression), ADHD, and behavioral problems in children whose mothers had higher prenatal stress.[4]

THERE ARE ALSO the spiritual components to consider, many of which are a result of physical impacts. The enemy is after your baby's soul from day one. Soul wounds can start in utero, whether from the stress of an unwanted pregnancy, hearing parents constantly fight, or being affected during an especially fearful birth process (C-sections, being born prematurely and separated from their mother's embrace, or pulled out forcefully with forceps).

Women have asked me if I believe the medical system is influenced by demonic forces. The answer is both yes and no. It's not always the case, as the Lord can use any situation for good. However, I do think the enemy feeds off of fear and anxiety, which is commonplace in the mainstream maternity system and in how most decisions are made. This pushes certain medical interventions during birth, which can affect the mother's journey beyond the immediate situation.

---

problems," *Proceedings of the National Academy of Sciences of the United States of America* 109, no. 20 (2012): E1312–E1319, https://www.pnas.org/doi/10.1073/pnas.1201295109.

3. M. S. Tollenaar, R. Beijers, J. Jansen, J. M. A. Riksen-Walraven, and C. de Weerth, "Maternal Prenatal Stress and Cortisol Reactivity to Stressors in Human Infants," *Stress* 14, no. 1 (2011): 53–65, https://doi.org/10.3109/10253890.2010.499485.

4. K. O'Donnell, T. G. O'Connor, and V. Glover, "Prenatal Stress and Neurodevelopment of the Child: Focus on the HPA Axis and Role of the Placenta," *Developmental Neuroscience* 31, no. 4 (2009): 285–292, https://doi.org/10.1159/000216539.

For example, if a doctor suggests a C-section due to fear, this decision affects many other factors. It influences hormonal balance, how a mother feels, and the physical and mental well-being of the baby. I believe a spiritual influence is at play here; if the enemy can control our minds, it will impact the physical world and have spiritual consequences.

Trauma during birth can also leave women hesitant about having more children, which I see as a form of spiritual warfare. The enemy desires to prevent women from having children because, when carrying a child, a woman holds the promise of fulfilling God's plans. There is a clear spiritual agenda behind discouraging women from becoming mothers.

A SPIRITUAL LESSON

Circling back to my experiences with spiritual warfare during pregnancy, at this point, you've heard about how, during my third pregnancy, I was told I had low progesterone. Initially, upon receiving this news, I felt a sense of peace and believed everything would be fine; however, I agreed to have my blood drawn again to check if my progesterone levels had risen, as my midwife suggested. Unfortunately, my results showed that my progesterone had actually decreased. This was when doubt began to creep in and when the spiritual battle reached its peak.

I was told that if I didn't supplement with synthetic progesterone to raise my levels, I could be at risk for a late pregnancy loss. I was even cautioned that natural progesterone options might not be sufficient to save my baby. What was spoken over me was, "If you don't take progesterone, you are setting yourself up for a late loss." As I absorbed this information, I began to feel dread, which quickly turned into panic.

Over the next several days, I struggled with intense anxiety. I started to question whether I was facing spiritual warfare or if this was a warning from God.

I cried, prayed, and asked God for direction: "Is this you, God? Are you trying to warn me? Where are you in all of this?" In response, I felt Him gently asking, "Is this how a warning from me would really feel?"

With a complete absence of peace, I realized that this pressure was not from Him. I made the decision to reject what I was told about my pregnancy and believe I am healed. After that, I threw away the prescribed progesterone and continued with my pregnancy.

Now, I'm not suggesting this is the path anyone else should take with a similar or the same diagnosis, but I want to share this very relevant, pivotal moment in my pregnancy that brought me closer to God.

I want to share this experience because, although I'm unsure if it was a ploy from the enemy or if my midwife simply did not realize the distress this would cause, I know that the enemy can take our circumstances and feed us lies. Satan is described as the father of lies (John 8:44), and the more we entertain his lies, the greater the anxiety and fear we experience.

From this experience, I gained a valuable perspective on how to discern whether something is from God. I learned to listen for God's voice and recognize the voice of the enemy. God's warnings are clear, peaceful, and purposeful.

For example, God warned Joseph in dreams to take Mary as his wife and later instructed him to flee to Egypt with baby Jesus. These warnings came with clear instructions, accompanied by peace and protection, not panic (Matthew 1:20; 2:13). Initially, when I learned about my progesterone levels, I felt at peace and sensed the Holy Spirit reassuring me that everything was fine. However, after choosing to undergo further testing, I allowed fear to take hold. Upon receiving the troubling news, fear flooded in, seemingly opening the door for the enemy to inject panic and confusion into my mind.

This contrast between God's clear, peaceful warnings and the enemy's chaos became apparent. When God warns, it is filled with wisdom, direction, and peace, even when urgent. If peace is absent, it's essential to evaluate the situation. Anxiety accompanied by confusion, shame, or a lack of clear next steps is not from God. I find comfort in the scripture, *"Let the peace of Christ rule in your hearts, since as members of one body you were called to peace. And be thankful"* (Colossians 3:15 NIV).

Although I was advised to take synthetic progesterone, I felt something was wrong and didn't know what steps to take. The direction I received felt unclear and confusing, which made me question whether it was truly God's guidance.

On the other hand, when I sought God's wisdom about what to do if I really did have low progesterone, I began to explore natural ways to increase my levels. This process brought clarity and peace, and I soon felt that I had clear steps to follow. In that moment of seeking, I found comfort and a sense of peace in my decision to not move forward with medication but to stand in faith. I feel it's important to share that standing in faith does not mean inaction. There were things I learned I could do to support my body while also trusting God with the outcome (James 2:14).

In contrast, the anxiety from the enemy is vague, heavy, and draining.

In Genesis 3:1–6, we see how Satan created confusion and fear by twisting God's word and exaggerating consequences. As a result, Eve made a fearful choice instead of a faithful one. The enemy's tactics have always been the same: to steal our peace, cloud our trust in God, and compel us to act out of panic instead of prayer.

I find comfort in the scripture that says, *"For God has not given us a spirit of fear and timidity, but a spirit of power, love, and self-discipline."* (2 Timothy 1:7 NLT). Whenever we experience anxiety that disrupts our peace or undermines our trust in God, we can be assured that it does not come from Him.

I am grateful it didn't take me long to realize that making decisions out of fear and panic wasn't the right approach. However, it's important to note that my situation, such as receiving a medical diagnosis, may look different for someone else. For instance, someone else could receive a similar message about low progesterone, be advised to take medication, and feel completely at peace with that decision.

The key point here is to evaluate your reaction to the information, not the information itself. God *invites* us to make choices, while the enemy pressures us. The Holy Spirit has made it clear to me that His guidance is gentle. As stated in Psalm 23:1–3, He leads us like a gentle shepherd. When God places a concern on your heart, whether it's about a birth plan or a healthcare provider, He does so gently. Although there can be urgency, it is never accompanied by shame, panic, or dread.

Conversely, the enemy often whispers things like, *You're not safe*, *You're not prepared*, or *Time is running out.* I felt this way when I thought I needed to make a decision immediately, fearing for my baby's safety. In those moments, I realized that those thoughts were not from God.

While there may be urgency in God's prompting, it is always gentle, without overwhelming pressure or fear. God speaks through peaceful nudges rather than fear-based impulses. It's essential to ask yourself: *Does anxiety push me toward prayer or panic? Does it make me run to God or try to control everything on my own? Is it accompanied by clarity or chaos?*

FROM GOD	FROM THE ENEMY
Peaceful warning	Panic and torment
Leads to clarity and next steps	Feeds confusion and dread
Strengthens your trust in God	Weakens your trust and peace
Prompts prayer and surrender	Prompts control and fear-based action
Encourages protection and wisdom	Produces overthinking and mental fog

It's completely normal to feel moments of concern during pregnancy; it's part of our hardwiring as mothers to care for our children from day one. However, when anxiety starts to rob you of your joy, cloud your thoughts, or create distance between you and God, it may actually be a sign of spiritual warfare rather than God's warnings. Remember James 1:5, which tells us that if we lack wisdom, we should ask God, and He will generously give it to us. So, if you're uncertain about whether a feeling is from God, take a moment to pause, ask Him for guidance, and wait for His peace to lead you.

Walking through pregnancy has given me a new perspective and has shown me where I have not taken God's Word for what it says. Yes, feelings are very real, but feelings are not the truth. As I have navigated discerning God's voice, the most important piece has been knowing what God's Word says to begin with and specifically understanding my identity in Christ under the full gospel. We are never wrong about any situation when we quote God and follow what He says. You are redeemed from the power of sin (Romans 6:14), healed in your soul, body, and spirit (Isaiah 53:5), no longer under Satan's authority or subject to things like fear and anxiety (Colossians 1:13), blessed and inherited (Galatians 3:13-14), empowered by the Holy Spirit (Acts 1:8), and an overcomer (Revelation 12:11).

QUESTIONS FOR REFLECTION

1. What scriptures help remind me that God always has good plans for me? (Take note of them.)
2. How often do I pause to compare my thoughts and feelings with what God's Word actually says before taking action?
3. What practical steps can I take daily to ensure God's Word is the foundation of my decisions and my peace during pregnancy?

4

WALKING BY THE SPIRIT AND THE PROCESS OF SURRENDERING

How can we actually walk by the Spirit of God during a time like pregnancy? A supercharged, emotional, and vulnerable time? A time when it's extremely easy to be swayed by our emotions and flesh? A time when the enemy can attack us? I shared my experience with progesterone during my third pregnancy and how I chose not to agree with the negative information surrounding it. I chose to believe that my body and my baby were healthy. I chose to believe God's word over my emotions.

This was a conscious decision, an act of faith. As I navigated this choice, I felt I was walking by the Spirit of God rather than being led by my emotions, fear, and anxiety. But was that enough for me to make a decision and move forward?

Not quite. I want to explain what it truly means to walk by the Spirit of God during pregnancy, how to do it, and how to actively surrender. Walking by the Spirit involves daily dependence on God's voice, guidance, power, and His word.

It's not about being perfect or convincing yourself that everything is fine; it's about being sensitive and surrendering. It's also important to clarify that walking by the Spirit, trusting God, and actively surrendering your pregnancy to Him does not mean rejecting medicine, medical treatment, or care. Choosing medical help doesn't make you any less holy or trusting in God.

Within the Christian community, I've noticed two extreme views. On one side, some believe that all doctors and medicine are gifts from God that should be fully embraced, while others completely demonize medicine and believe it goes against God's design.

I believe that some forms of medicine can be blessings, and I'm thankful to God for allowing us to discover medical advancements, including surgical options when needed. However, I also believe that God designed our bodies to heal themselves and that medicine is often overused, particularly during pregnancy and childbirth. I think we should first rely on natural methods of healing whenever possible and ultimately see God as our Healer.

THE HOLY SPIRIT, MY ULTIMATE GUIDE

Now, regarding my experiences during pregnancy, the information I received, and the things that were spoken over me, how did I remain sensitive to God's voice throughout this journey? How did I lean on His guidance above all else?

I want to share what walking by the Spirit has looked like for me during my pregnancy. To walk in step with the Spirit while pregnant means to ask questions before reacting, to surrender before spiraling, to listen before striving, and to prioritize peace over panic. It means following God's wisdom and Word instead of succumbing to cultural pressures.

Galatians 5:16 captures this sentiment: Walk by the Spirit, not the flesh. It's about tuning into the Holy Spirit before responding to emotions. Instead of letting anxiety compel you to overthink and try to fix everything yourself, the Spirit of God encourages you to pause, pray, and listen.

When fear, doubt, or stress arises, you can pray, "Holy Spirit, lead me. I don't want to make decisions out of fear." Respond to all emotions with prayer instead of panic. Remember, pregnancy hormones like progesterone and estrogen can amplify emotional responses, making your brain more sensitive and reactive (yes, pregnancy is spiritual, but there are still physical impacts we need to be aware of).

But God's Spirit offers a peace that surpasses all understanding (Philippians 4:7). When you take a moment to pray, you calm your nervous system and shift from reaction to reliance. You're training both your brain and your developing baby's nervous system to respond with peace rather than panic.

Nourishing your body during this time should be viewed as an act of worship. Your flesh might say, *I deserve to indulge; I feel awful, so I'll eat whatever I want.* But the Spirit of God reminds you that your body is a temple and you should steward it with love.

You can ask the Holy Spirit, "Would you nourish me today? What does my baby need from me in love?" This approach doesn't lead to such things as legalism or guilt over food choices; instead, it invites God into all aspects of your pregnancy. Remember, what you eat can affect your mood, energy, and even your baby's development.

Stable blood sugar levels contribute to a stable mood. Nutrients like magnesium, omega-3 fatty acids, and B vitamins play an essential role in supporting emotional health and hormonal balance. Additionally, natural, whole foods help reduce inflammation, which is often linked to anxiety and fatigue. When you intentionally nourish your body, you are caring for your temple and sowing seeds of vitality for both yourself and your baby.

Walking by the Spirit may include slowing down and saying no when needed. Your flesh might tell you, *I have to push through; I can't stop now.* However, the Spirit of God invites you to rest. Jesus is not asking you to hustle. Allow the Spirit to lead you into a restful state that is not laziness, but rather holy stillness.

During pregnancy, your body's energy demands increase; your heart pumps more blood, your metabolism rises, and your body is continuously at work. Chronic stress elevates cortisol levels, which can impact your baby's brain and emotional development. Taking time to rest helps stimulate hormones, improve immune function, and reduce inflammation. God designed the Sabbath for man. Rest is not a sign of laziness; it's an act of obedience.

Your flesh may urge you to follow what the world deems safest, but the Spirit of God encourages you to seek His guidance on what is best. Remember, He knows your body and your baby intimately. Present each doctor's recommendation to the Lord in prayer. Ask God, "Is this the direction You have for me and this birth?" This is where faith meets discernment.

He will grant you peace as you pursue His path for your journey. While professional wisdom is valuable, not all advice is Spirit-led, and every pregnancy is unique. God knows your individual story.

Finally, speak life over your womb. Your flesh might whisper fears like, *I'm scared something bad will happen*, but the Spirit of God encourages you to declare His Word and truth over your womb. Affirm life and truth every single day. *God is knitting this baby together, and I will not fear bad news. My heart is steady, trusting in the Lord.* As Psalm 112:7 says, speaking life can change the spiritual atmosphere and strengthen your faith.

Walking by the Spirit of God does not mean ignoring everything around us. Instead, it involves using the Word of God and the Holy Spirit as our Counselor and guide to make decisions rooted in peace and truth rather than fear.

WHAT SURRENDER CAN LOOK LIKE

If you're wondering how to truly surrender something to God, you may want to know what that looks like in practice. Surrendering can sometimes feel challenging, so here are some practical ways to surrender to God.

1. Communicate with God honestly. As 1 Peter 5:7 (NLT) says, *"Give all your worries and cares to God, for he cares about you."* Rather than suppressing your fears, bring them into the light through prayer. Say things like, "Lord, I feel scared, but I choose to trust You. Help my unbelief. Show me what to do."
2. Take every thought captive. As instructed in 2 Corinthians 10:5 (NLT), *"We destroy every proud obstacle that keeps people from knowing God. We capture their rebellious thoughts and teach them to obey Christ."* Surrender begins with vulnerability, not performance. When thoughts of fear, control, or "what-ifs" arise, write them down. Lay them before the Lord in prayer and replace them with truth-based affirmations. For instance, remind yourself that God formed this baby and holds your future, as stated in Psalm 139 and Jeremiah 29:11.
3. Physical posture can change a spiritual posture. Physical posture matters; it can remind your body to surrender as well. I found it helpful during my own surrenders. Try praying on your knees or with your hands open, saying, "Not my will, but Yours be done. I release control. I receive Your peace."
4. Meditate on scriptures daily. Faith comes by hearing the Word (Romans 10:17). Each week, choose one to two verses that focus on themes of surrender, peace, or God's promises for motherhood. For example: *"You will keep in perfect peace all who trust in you, all whose thoughts are fixed on you!" "You keep in perfect peace those whose minds are stayed on you"* (Isaiah 26:3 NLT and ESV) and *"Be still and know that I am God"* (Psalm 46:10 NIV). Allow God to renew your mind through His Word. Lay down control one decision at a time. Ask God, "Is there anything You want me to do or release?"

5. Worship during moments of anxiety. Worship realigns your spirit to the truth, and fear cannot exist in a place filled with praise. Turn on the worship music and open your mouth with praise to God.
6. Invite others in. Don't hesitate to ask others for prayer. Inviting community into your journey is an act of surrender, as you are expressing that you don't have to be strong on your own. Let a trusted friend or mentor intercede for you when you feel weary. I experienced this during my third pregnancy when I received news that made me want to spiral. I approached my community of fellow believers and shared my feelings. This made me feel vulnerable, as many view me as an expert in pregnancy and birth and believe I shouldn't have fears or worries. However, that act was part of my surrendering process, acknowledging that I am not perfect and do face my own issues and fears about pregnancy.

Surrendering does not mean doing nothing; it means acting only on His guidance. For instance, surrender your fear regarding ultrasounds, birth plans, or diagnoses. Choose not to spiral into anxiety by seeking second opinions online unless God prompts you to do so, and do this not out of fear.

Remember, surrender is not giving up; it is giving over. It doesn't mean pretending that everything is easy. Instead, it means living from the truth of God's word and knowing that He is the one carrying the weight.

QUESTIONS FOR REFLECTION

1. Have I fully invited God into every part of this pregnancy, physically, emotionally, and spiritually?

2. Am I trusting God with the timing, development, and outcome of my pregnancy, or am I trying to control it?
3. What fears am I holding on to that I haven't laid at the feet of Jesus?
4. Do I believe that God is forming this baby with intention and purpose, even when things feel uncertain?
5. Am I looking to the world or to the Word to define what a good pregnancy should be like?
6. When fear arises, is my first instinct to pray or Google?
7. Am I nurturing my body in a way that honors the life God is creating within me?
8. How often do I pause to ask, "Holy Spirit, what are you saying to me today about this pregnancy?
9. What expectations do I need to release so I can receive what God has for me in this season?
10. Do I believe that God is not just with me in this pregnancy, but that He chose me for this baby and this season?

PART 2

HOLY CHILDBIRTH, THE REFINER'S FIRE

Lord, you are the Author of Life and the Creator of my body. I thank you for designing birth with intention, beauty, and purpose.
I reject fear and receive your peace. I reject the lie that birth is cursed, and I embrace the truth that through Jesus, I am redeemed. Teach me to trust the way you designed this process, leaning into your strength rather than my own.
May my labor be led by your Spirit, and may my birth be a testimony of your goodness. I invite you into every contraction, every breath, and every moment. Be glorified in the miracle of the life you are bringing forth.
In Jesus's name, amen.

5

GOD'S DESIGN FOR BIRTH

So far, we have discussed the call to surrender during the season of pregnancy, the first step in accepting the Lord's holy invitation to say yes to His Kingdom plans and assignments as mothers. Surrendering during pregnancy leads to the defining moment you have been preparing for over the last ten months: the birth of your baby.

Our culture has injected so much fear into this space. What I have observed is that the enemy has been at work for generations, trying to twist the truth about God's plan for His daughters concerning childbirth.

God's birth plans emphasize faith over fear, surrender over struggle, peace over pain, worship over worry, confidence over chaos, trust over tension, and blessings over burdens. But let's start from the beginning. One of the most commonly asked questions is, "Didn't God curse women to experience painful childbirth?"

This is the first topic I want to unpack. There are some mistaken theological arguments surrounding childbirth. The first is the notion that you are guaranteed a birth without struggle or pain. The second is the belief that if you receive any interventions, like an epidural during childbirth, you are not submitting to the pain that God wants you to endure.

So, what is the truth? What does God desire for His daughters in a broken world?

We must go back to Genesis, to the fall. The brokenness of the world resulting from the fall still affects us as women. Hardship on our journey to motherhood may occur, but not because God necessarily wants us to struggle. Genesis 3:16 (NIV) states, "*To the woman he said, 'I will make your pains in childbearing very severe; with painful labor, you will give birth to children.*'" Other translations say, "*I will intensify your labor pains. You will bear children with painful effort*" (CSB).

What God is communicating here is the impact of the fall. Adam and Eve sinned together. They did this due to distrust and the desire to be like God, despite already being created in His image.

God then curses the ground and the serpent, intentionally setting them apart for complete destruction. As you read the Bible in its entirety, through the book of Revelation, you will see that two things are ultimately destroyed: the earth and the dragon (or serpent). Importantly, God does not curse the woman or the man.

However, He acknowledges the effects of the fall on their labor. The Hebrew word used for Adam's labor in producing fruit from the ground is the same one used when God states, "*I will greatly increase your labor in childbirth.*"

The Hebrew nouns "*itziban*" and "*etzeb*" stem from the root "*atzav,*" which carries a range of meanings, including toil, hardship, sorrow, and emotional anguish, not strictly physical pain. It's important to understand the context: Adam was to produce life from the ground, while Eve was to produce life from her womb. In an agrarian society, this would have been easily understood by those reading this scripture.

What God is really saying is, "Because you chose to sin, because you chose the opposite of me, this is what will happen to you." Their disobedience resulted in increased labor, encompassing the entire reproductive process, not just birth itself. For example, infertility or miscarriage can also be seen as labor pains. We have increased "labor pains" throughout the reproductive process due to the disobedience of Adam, which functionally handed over authority to Satan and made him the ruler of this world (John 12:31). Satan causes pain, death, and destruction, not God.

But here's the good news: Jesus came as the last Adam (1 Corinthians 15:45). Where the first Adam lost authority through disobedience, Jesus regained authority through perfect obedience. After the resurrection, Jesus declares, *"All authority in heaven and on earth has been given to Me"* (Matthew 28:18, NLT). That's the reversal. Jesus didn't just defeat Satan; He stripped him of all his power: *"He disarmed the powers and authorities and made a public spectacle of them"* (Colossians 2:15). Jesus then goes on to say, *"I have given you authority ... to overcome all the power of the enemy"* (Luke 10:19). He's talking about the believer.

You are not cursed, and your body is not cursed, but we do know that birth, as a whole, has been affected by the fall. God does not intend for you to feel agonizing pain during labor, although pain may occur. While Christ redeemed us from the curse of the law by becoming a curse for us, this does not guarantee that we will experience life without hardship or pain. However, as believers, we must enforce our authority through resisting the devil (James 4:7), taking every thought captive (2 Corinthians 10:3–5), binding and loosing into our atmosphere (Matthew 18:18), and declaring what Christ already secured.

God has good plans for women. Although He is not directly referred to as a midwife in scripture, some verses contain strong parallels to midwifery, especially concerning the act of bringing forth life and assisting during birth. For example, *"Yet you brought me safely from my mother's womb and led me to trust you at my mother's breast."* (Psalm 22:9 NLT). This implies God's active role in bringing forth life from the womb, like a divine midwife attending a birth.

In Isaiah 66:9 (NLT), the Lord says, *"'Would I ever bring this nation to the point of birth and then not deliver it?' asks the Lord. 'No! I would never keep this nation from being born,' says your God."* Here, God compares Himself to the one overseeing birth, ensuring that what He initiates He also brings to completion, much like a midwife who sees a delivery through. This speaks to God's heart for women during childbirth.

THE BEAUTY OF HIS BLUEPRINT

So, what is His design for birth? Essentially, God's design reflects how He created our bodies as women to give birth. It is that simple.

If we set aside everything we've been told or thought about birth, we can see the basic function of our bodies in this process. Believe it or not, God did not design epidurals; humans did. Epidurals are a tool created to assist with labor, but they were not part of God's original design. I want to return to that original design: our physiology.

What is physiology? By definition, it refers to the normal functions of living organisms and their parts. I want to emphasize the word "normal." Birth, therefore, is something our bodies know how to do; it's a normal function, like using the bathroom, and does not need to be taught.

God's design, the physiology of birth, unfolds best when it is allowed to progress without intervention. To illustrate this, think about using the bathroom: if someone walked in while you were trying to go, offering advice, making loud noises, or coaching you on how to push, how would that feel? You might feel blocked or unable to go at all. This highlights how hormonal processes in our bodies can be affected by external factors.

I share this to help you understand how God designed our bodies. His creation and design are incredible. We know that God's heart for childbirth is loving; He never cursed women, nor did He intend for childbirth to be unbearably painful, as the world perceives it. When I reflect on God's design for birth, I see it as a blessing, not a burden.

In the Bible, the term "burden" is defined in several ways: as a load of any kind (Exodus 23:5), a severe task (Exodus 2:11), a difficult duty (Exodus 18:22), and a prophecy of calamity or disaster (Isaiah 18:1). Synonyms include anxiety, concern, difficulty, load, strain, trouble, punishment, hindrance, excess, baggage, trial, and misfortune. In contrast, antonyms include calmness, contentment, blessing, ease, happiness, praise, encouragement, help, relief, and benefit.

In scripture, Jesus says, "*Come to me, all who labor and are heavy laden, and I will give you rest. Take my yoke upon you, and learn from me; for I am gentle and lowly in heart, and you will find rest for your souls. For my yoke is easy, and my burden is light*" (Matthew 11:28–30 ESV). The yoke Jesus speaks of is a free gift that requires willing submission and leads us to a posture of surrender and trust.

God's design for birth aligns with His work. Therefore, it's important to understand how intricately He designed us so we can cooperate with our bodies rather than work against them.

God created a perfect symphony of hormones in our bodies. When allowed to unfold naturally and undisturbed, childbirth doesn't have to be unbearably painful and can proceed smoothly. This is part of God's design. Now, hang in there with me, as I want to dive into the physiology of birth and just how important God's design is.

Each hormone serves a specific purpose. Oxytocin, for example, is God's natural way of progressing labor and fostering a bond between you and your baby. Endorphins act as your body's built-in pain relief, helping you cope and even experience euphoria.

Adrenaline provides a surge of alertness and strength when it's time to bring your baby into your arms. Prolactin prepares you to care for and feed your baby while also promoting a relaxed, focused state that helps you tune into your baby's needs, even during labor. Relaxin softens your body to facilitate birth, and melatonin, which works with oxytocin, helps create a calm, steady flow during labor.

The stages of birth, reflecting God's miraculous design, begin with early labor. During this phase, the cervix softens, thins (effaces), and begins to open. Gentle, wavelike contractions occur in the uterus, allowing your baby to move deeper into the pelvis.

Oxytocin, God's natural hormone for love and labor, begins to work mildly, triggering rhythmic contractions. Relaxin softens the cervix and loosens ligaments, opening the pelvis. Melatonin, which works best at night, is one reason many women go into labor naturally during this time; it helps oxytocin flow in sync and keeps labor calm.

Next comes active labor, where the cervix continues to dilate. Uterine contractions become stronger, longer, and more frequent, drawing the cervix open. At this stage, the baby moves into an optimal position, guided by the contractions and your body's movements. The effect of oxytocin increases the power of these stronger contractions.

Endorphin levels continue to rise to help your body cope with the intensity. God's pain relief is specifically designed for labor. Melatonin helps maintain a peaceful flow of labor, especially in a dark, quiet environment. Remember, your uterus is the strongest muscle in your body, and it knows exactly what to do. As pressure builds during labor, so does your body's natural pain relief, proving that God does not abandon you in difficulty; rather, He provides strength during labor.

You then move into the transition phase. The cervix will finish dilating to ten centimeters, allowing your baby to descend. This is the most intense part of labor, characterized by quick, powerful contractions with little rest in between. You may feel shaky and emotional or even want to give up; these reactions are normal signs that the baby is near. Throughout this time, oxytocin surges to complete dilation. Endorphins peak to help your mind transcend the intensity, and adrenaline kicks in to prepare your body for pushing and to increase your energy and alertness.

The final stage is pushing and giving birth to your baby, with the uterus contracting to guide the baby down through the birth canal. You'll feel an urge to bear down, a reflex triggered by your baby's position and pressure. As the baby is born, adrenaline sharpens your focus and provides you with the strength to push. Oxytocin continues to contract the uterus and facilitates the bonding process as soon as your baby arrives.

After the birth, the final stage is delivering the placenta. The uterus contracts to expel the placenta, and the blood vessels seal to prevent excessive bleeding. The uterus begins to shrink and firm up while skin-to-skin contact and breastfeeding begin. Your baby instinctively seeks the breast, as God designed. This increases oxytocin levels, which helps contract the uterus and initiate bonding and breastfeeding.

Prolactin prepares your body to nourish your baby, both physically and emotionally, while endorphins fill you with love and, possibly, tears. The same hormone that made labor intense now brings forth an overflow of love. Birth does not just end with the arrival of a baby; it initiates a bond. God crafted every hormone to transition you from warrior to nurturer in a sacred, seamless way.

God designed this process perfectly, and while we have explored why childbirth may require pain and labor from a theological perspective, one might wonder if there is a purpose behind these experiences designed by God. During labor, waves of contractions of varying intensity play a meaningful role.

He developed this process to effectively deliver our babies from the womb while allowing us to rest during the journey. During a contraction, the uterus experiences a tightening, which builds the fundus (the top of the uterus) and opens the cervix.

Contractions are highly productive, and when you view them through an understanding of how your body functions as God designed it, your perspective shifts from *What is happening to me?* to *This is an effective and productive process.* So, why are these sensations valuable during labor?

Pain serves as guidance. It helps the mother know when to move, breathe, rest, or push. Pain provides real-time feedback from the body.

Furthermore, pain and/or sensation increase bonding. Experiencing contractions releases oxytocin, the hormone responsible for love and connection between mother and baby. Pain can also lead to a sense of surrender.

Pain humbles the mother, drawing her into a deeper reliance on God's strength rather than relying solely on her own. It also serves as a form of communication; labor pain is how the mother and baby interact with each other.

Each contraction helps the baby move, and the mother responds to the baby's needs. Additionally, pain refines us; much like how fire purifies gold, labor pain is part of a spiritual process that shapes and sanctifies the mother. I can personally attest to this.

THE GAP BETWEEN GOD'S DESIGN AND MODERN BIRTH

This all sounds wonderful, right? So, why aren't more women aware of this design? Why do so many women fear childbirth? Why are so many women experiencing unnecessary birth trauma? This leads to the question: why is God's design different from modern birth culture? The distinction lies in trust: trust in the Creator versus trust in the system.

Modern culture heavily relies on the medical system, interventions, and man-made timelines. There's more trust in experts than in the Creator. However, birth was designed by God; He created a woman's body to grow and deliver life through His power and wisdom. God's design teaches that birth is a blessing and an honor, a partnership with Him in bringing new life forth.

Though the world views birth as a painful inconvenience to be avoided or merely endured, it should be seen as a sacred encounter. It is a matter of surrendering to God's timing, strength, and peace versus attempting to control the situation.

Modern culture promotes control through scheduling inductions, managing pain with interventions, and striving to oversee every outcome, which often diminishes spiritual dependence on God.

Holistic preparation is essential, as God's design involves preparing the heart, body, and spirit. Pregnancy is a time for spiritual growth and sanctification, whereas modern culture often emphasizes superficial preparations, focusing on gear, apps, and surface-level concerns while neglecting the soul and spirit.

Identity is also crucial: you are a daughter of God, not defined by labels or risk factors. Your identity is secure in God.

In contrast, modern culture assigns labels like "high risk" or "geriatric pregnancy," conditioning women to expect limitations during their pregnancies and childbirth experiences.

The journey of birth is one where faith overcomes fear. Fear has no place in the presence of God's love; His perfect love casts out fear (1 John 4:18). However, modern culture is steeped in fear: fear of pain, complications, failure, and trauma.

The world often tells women to expect the worst and be surprised if things go well. So, what are the true impacts of modern birth culture on the birthing experience, specifically on God's design for birth?

When you experience fear, your adrenaline and cortisol levels spike (remember all those beautiful hormones God designed that we just covered?). This heightened state causes tension in the body, which can actually lead to pain; this is by design.

Interestingly, feeling fear can prolong or stall labor, functioning as a protective mechanism. This is why feeling safe during labor is so important.

Adrenaline and cortisol restrict oxygen to the uterus and redirect it to larger muscle groups, preparing the mother to flee from danger. Many mothers report progressing well in labor at home, but once they head to the hospital, their labor may slow down or stall. This is likely because the mother feels less safe or more uncomfortable in that environment.

This response is a natural part of God's design for the body. The pervasive fear surrounding childbirth can have significant physical impacts, and it's also reflected in various statistics. For instance, the

U.S. maternal mortality rate has more than doubled from 2000 to 2021, and the country has the highest maternal mortality rate among high-income nations.[1] Additionally, there are higher rates of C-sections and medical interventions, as well as a healthcare system that prioritizes emergency care over preventative maternal wellness.[2]

Furthermore, up to 45% of mothers report experiencing some form of birth trauma and feeling deeply distressed by their delivery experience, with a diagnosis of PTSD affecting about 4% to 6% of birthing women. Meanwhile, 12% to 17% of women experience post-traumatic stress symptoms after delivery.[3,4] Clearly, this is not what God intended.

As more women suffer from negative childbirth experiences, the modern culture of fear and control surrounding birth continues to perpetuate itself. It's a repeating cycle: fear and societal norms have led many to believe that hospitals are the safest places to give birth. However, when you look at the statistics, the truth is striking: about 98.4% of women give birth in hospitals, and despite this, we are still seeing concerning maternal mortality rates, as well as high C-section rates, with approximately 33% of women having them.[5,6] That means one in every three women will have a C-section.

---

1. Justina Petrullo, "US Has Highest Infant, Maternal Mortality Rates Despite the Most Health Care Spending," *The American Journal of Managed Care* (January 31, 2023), https://www.ajmc.-com/view/us-has-highest-infant-maternal-mortality-rates-despite-the-most-health-care-spending.
2. Petrullo, "US Has Highest Infant, Maternal Mortality Rates."
3. Cara Goodwin, Ph.D., "What Is Trauma, and How Common Is It? What Birth Trauma Is, How to Know if You've Experienced It, and the Impacts," *Psychology Today*, May 22, 2023, https://www.psychologytoday.com/us/blog/parenting-translator/202305/what-is-birth-trauma-and-how-common-is-it
4. Mia Hemstad, *Birth Trauma and Maternal Mental Health Fact Sheet*, Maternal Mental Health Leadership Alliance, September 7, 2023, https://www.mmhla.org/articles/birth-trauma-and-maternal-mental-health-fact-sheet/.
5. National Academies of Sciences, Engineering, and Medicine, *Maternal and Newborn Care in the United States*, in *Birth Settings in America: Outcomes, Quality, Access, and Choice*, ed. E. P. Backes and S. C. Scrimshaw (Washington, DC: National Academies Press [US], 2020), https://www.ncbi.nlm.nih.gov/books/NBK555484/.
6. Chunhui Lai et al., "Effect of Different Delivery Modes on Intestinal Microbiota and Immune Function of Neonates," *Scientific Reports* **14** (2024): Article 17452, https://www.nature.com/articles/s41598-024-68599-x.

Some people might hear this and think it's not that significant. But when you take a holistic view and examine how mothers are actually doing, it raises important questions. Why do so many women experience postpartum anxiety and depression? Why do so many face challenges with breastfeeding? These issues run much deeper than just the outcome of birth.

The location of birth, hospital versus home, may not matter as much as the interventions that take place during a hospital birth. The issues stem from the fact that we are going against God's design.

In many cases, interventions that go against God's perfectly designed physiological process are normalized. Many say, "Oh, I'm just going to get induced; it's no big deal," or "They're just going to give me this during labor." The notion of having a C-section has become commonplace, but that's not the design intended for childbirth. I would like to say that just because a C-section is not part of God's original design, it does not mean it cannot be helpful and life-saving at times.

However, when you go through the natural processes of labor as designed, the hormones involved affect postpartum recovery, your baby, and your overall experience as a mother. We cannot ignore this fact. The impact is profound: physically, mentally, and spiritually. I want to unpack some examples of this.

For instance, consider the physiological design behind childbirth. During vaginal delivery, the baby passes through the birth canal and is exposed to beneficial gut flora and vaginal flora. This is crucial for building their gut microbiome, which serves as the foundation of their immune system from day one.[7] With C-sections, babies miss out on this important benefit that God intended.

Continuous monitoring during labor has also become the cultural norm, where women are strapped to machines to monitor their babies constantly (despite this not being based on any evidence proving that it improves birth outcomes). This practice is often seen as safer than

7. Zhang et al., "The Effects of Delivery Mode on the Gut Microbiota and Health."

allowing mothers the freedom to move and connect with their bodies and babies throughout labor.[8] However, it's important to recognize that God's design emphasizes the physical and hormonal connection between a mother and her child.

Additionally, the common image of childbirth is a woman lying on her back and being directed to push. This method goes against how our bodies are designed to function optimally. Upright positions, where the pelvis can open and allow the baby to descend with gravity, are much more effective.[9]

The separation of mothers and babies after birth has also become normalized. We often hear about cutting the cord immediately after birth, but it's important to recognize that there is intentionality and design behind this process that pours into a woman's postpartum experience and impacts her baby.

The bonding hormones generated immediately after birth play a huge role in the following days, weeks, and months, and we do not want to cut this off. The baby continues to receive oxygen, blood, and stem cells from the mother's placenta as well. However, in our current society, it seems common to separate the mother and baby right after birth, without considering the natural design behind the process. Culturally, again, we tend to rely on controlling the situation.

As soon as the baby is placed on the mother's skin, it triggers the flow of oxytocin, which helps stop the mother's bleeding. Moreover, when the baby latches on for breastfeeding, it further increases oxytocin levels and aids in uterine contractions, all part of the natural design intended to help the mother heal.

We often hear about mothers experiencing hemorrhaging after

---

8. Lisa Heelan, "Fetal Monitoring: Creating a Culture of Safety With Informed Choice," *Journal of Perinatal Education* 22, no. 3 (2013): 156–165, https://www.ncbi.nlm.nih.gov/pmc/articles/PMC4010242/.

9. Rebecca Dekker, PhD, RN, "The Evidence on: Birthing Positions," *Evidence Based Birth®*, October 2, 2012 (updated July 11, 2022), https://www.evidencebasedbirth.com/evidence-birthing-positions/..

birth, which can, indeed, happen, but it's worth examining the circumstances surrounding it.[10] Was God's natural design disrupted?

I wanted to zoom out and share some examples of how modern society can go against God's design. Again, statistically, we can see that many women are not having positive experiences in childbirth, which points back to more fear around birth being created, as well as the impacts on mom and baby from missing out on God's design for this process.

The world has largely removed God from the birth experience, turning it into something filled with fear and burden, as if it is something we must endure or medicate through. But I'm here to share the truth about birth: it can be a blessing.

Childbirth does not need to be feared; it can be a joyful experience. I want everyone to encounter the divine kindness, mercy, and goodness that God has bestowed upon us through childbirth.

In the next chapter, we will explore how to practically follow God's design for birth, how to seek Him, surrender to Him, and be refined through it all.

QUESTIONS FOR REFLECTION

1. How have I viewed birth up to this point, and where might fear or misconceptions have influenced my mindset instead of God's truth?
2. How does understanding God's good blueprint for birth change the way I prepare mentally, spiritually, and emotionally for this moment?

10. Wedad M. Almutairi, "Literature Review: Physiological Management for Preventing Postpartum Hemorrhage," *Healthcare* 9, no. 6 (2021): 658, https://www.mdpi.com/2227-9032/9/6/658.

6

DESIGN TO LABOR

WORKING WITH GOD'S BLUEPRINT

After nearly ten months of pregnancy, preparing holistically, physically, mentally, and spiritually, you finally reach the day you go into labor. It's an exciting whirlwind of emotions, and truly, many feelings are involved.

Just as we discussed walking by the Spirit during pregnancy, we can also walk by the Spirit during birth. When the time comes, there's no better way to set the tone for your labor than to invite the Holy Spirit to continue guiding you according to God's blueprint for birth. I always say that God designed our bodies perfectly, so how can we work with them rather than against them during this process?

God didn't just create birth; He designed your body for it. When you honor that design, labor becomes less an ordeal to merely get through and more about partnering with God throughout the experience. To prepare for birth, start by inviting Him into the process.

God has carried you through pregnancy, and He wants to be involved in all areas of your life. In scripture, He tells us, *"I tell you, you can pray for anything, and if you believe that you've received it, it will be yours."* (Mark 11:24 NLT).

This scripture was particularly encouraging to me during pregnancy and the lead-up to my baby's birth because it opened my eyes to the fact that I could dream with God and ask Him to be part of the experience. I could even ask Him for specific things regarding my birth. While God isn't a genie, I believed that He would honor my requests just like He said.

So, what does this look like? What are some things I prayed for during my baby's birth? I prayed for the time of day my baby would be born. I prayed for peace during labor. I prayed for a quick pushing stage. I prayed that my water would not break until right before my baby was born because this can actually make labor more tolerable (the intact bag of water acts as a cushion to the cervix). I prayed my other children would be present but calm during my labor, and most of all, I prayed for God to be glorified throughout it all. I prayed that the birth would serve as a testimony of His faithfulness and open the eyes of an unbeliever to the reality of God.

I prayed with faith, believing that God would answer. I think many pregnant moms hesitate to ask God for specific things regarding their pregnancies, especially concerning the birth of their babies, because they fear disappointment. We often prefer not to ask to avoid potential hurt, even though God always answers; His answers may simply be different from what we expect. Some women might worry that asking God for something specific implies a desire to control the outcome, which feels counter to surrendering. They may think, *if I trust God, shouldn't I just say, "Your will be done," and leave it at that?*

However, biblically, God invites both surrender and bold asking, as seen in Philippians 4:6 and Matthew 7:7. Many women avoid specifics to escape the shame of feeling they "got it wrong" if everything doesn't unfold perfectly.

A great example is Jesus's own prayer in the Garden of Gethsemane: *"Father, if you are willing, take this cup of suffering away from me. Yet I want your will to be done, not mine."* (Luke 22:42 NLT). He prayed specifically while holding the outcome with open hands.

Here's what I've realized about God: He seeks glory, and by

answering our prayers, He brings Himself incredible honor. You can pray with faith and intentionally involve God in your birth planning with the goal of glorifying Him throughout the process. I encourage moms to pray boldly, surrender freely, and process everything honestly by bringing the planning back to God when needed.

The birth of my first child truly opened my eyes to the fact that we have a God who hears our prayers and cares about even the tiniest details of our lives. Just as an earthly father loves to spoil his child by giving good gifts, our Heavenly Father does the same. In Matthew 7:9-11, it states (paraphrasing), "If your children ask for a loaf of bread, do you give them a stone?... How much more will your heavenly Father give good gifts to those who ask Him?"

God desires for us to engage with Him, to pray without ceasing, and to ask for what we desire and need. This is actually a command from God. *"Always be joyful. Never stop praying. Be thankful in all circumstances, for this is God's will for you in Christ Jesus."* (1 Thessalonians 5:16–18) So, what might happen if we prayed during labor?

Prayer shifts your focus to God's peace, naturally increasing oxytocin levels. More oxytocin leads to stronger and more efficient contractions, resulting in a smoother labor experience. It also reduces stress, promoting calmness and bonding with your baby.

Prayer helps to lower cortisol, the stress hormone. High levels of cortisol can slow labor, increase pain perception, and create tension in the body. Lower cortisol means less tension in your muscles and a more comfortable labor experience.

Prayer also increases endorphins, which are our natural, God-designed painkillers. Engaging in prayer and worship can release waves of endorphins, making you feel more in control and less overwhelmed. Higher endorphin levels lead to a greater pain threshold, and there can even be moments of euphoria during labor.

I vividly remember my second labor when, just a couple of hours into it, I could sense that things were becoming very intense. My husband instinctively grabbed his Bible and began praying scripture over me. In that moment, it felt supernatural as a wave of peace washed over me. My focus shifted entirely to Jesus, and I felt a surge of strength.

This experience served as a powerful reminder that when we shift our focus from fear to the Father, our circumstances can change.

ANOINTING

There are several other practical ways to invite the Holy Spirit into your birthing process, tapping into His design and blueprint. Before giving birth to my second and third child, I anointed and dedicated the space to the Lord. Although anointing may seem symbolic, it aligns our brain, body, and spirit, activating faith, calming the nervous system, honoring God's design, and creating an atmosphere reminiscent of heaven for your baby's arrival.

Anointing with oil is mentioned multiple times in both the Old and New Testaments of the Bible. For example, Exodus 40:9 (NIV) says, *"Take the anointing oil and anoint the tabernacle and everything in it. Consecrate it and all its furnishings, and it will be holy."* In Genesis 28:18, Jacob pours oil on the stone he used as a pillow. Mark 6:13 states that the disciples drove out many demons and anointed many sick people with oil, healing them. James 5:14 NIV advises, *"Is anyone among you sick? Let them call the elders of the church to pray over them and anoint them with oil in the name of the Lord."*

The oil signifies various things, such as the presence of the Holy Spirit, and is also believed to possess sanctifying and cleansing properties. Oil serves as a symbol of healing, consecration, and authority, inviting the power of the Lord to move for healing, protection, and covering.

It's important to note that there's nothing magical about the oil; we perform this act in faith. Anointing is a prophetic act; it's a physical expression of a spiritual reality. During labor, fear, chaos, or spiritual attacks can intrude. However, when you dedicate your space to the Lord, it becomes a sanctuary of peace, worship, and strength.

Here's how to anoint your space:

1. Choose your oil. You can use olive oil or a pre-blessed anointing oil. You might also consider scents like frankincense or myrrh.
2. Pray over the oil, dedicating it to God for His purposes.
3. Invite the Holy Spirit and ask God to cleanse, sanctify, and fill the space with His peace and presence. You might pray something like: "Lord, I set this place apart for You. Let every inch of this room be filled with Your Spirit, peace, power, and protection. Let nothing unholy dwell here. May this room be filled with heavenly joy, supernatural strength, and the presence of Your angels."
4. Anoint key areas, such as doorways, as a symbolic act of keeping anything unclean or fearful out while welcoming God's presence.

By following these steps, you can create a spiritually nurturing environment for your labor.

Your bed or birthing tub is where you will labor physically, and it is important to anoint it for strength and peace. Oil on the walls and windows can symbolically cover the entire room, offering God's protection. You, your spouse, or your birth team can perform an anointing of your body, focusing on your belly, forehead, and hands, and declaring your body a vessel for God's glory during this birth. Rebuke any spirits and cancel any attacks against you and your baby that are not of God.

Here are some declarations that I like to use: "God rules in this space" (Colossians 3:15), "*No weapon formed against me shall prosper*" (Isaiah 54:17 KJV), and "The Lord goes before me and is my rear guard" (Isaiah 52:12). Anointing with oil has definite spiritual, emotional, and symbolic significance; it reinforces positive expectancy.

When you anoint with oil and pair it with worship, prayer, and affirmations, your brain forms strong, positive associations with the experience of birth. If you choose to use a scented oil, remember that smell is deeply linked to memory and emotion through our limbic system.

Anointing can also calm the stress response. This act helps shift your mental focus from *What if?* to *God is here* in faith. It activates and reinforces your parasympathetic nervous system, which is responsible for rest, digestion, and childbirth.

You are essentially rewiring your brain for peace. Additionally, scripture emphasizes the importance of affirming God's truth. "*Death and life are in the power of the tongue*" (Proverbs 18:21 KJV). What we speak doesn't just influence us emotionally; it can bring life or death into a situation.

Declare Scripture

Similar to anointing your space, you can read and declare scripture to invite the Lord and His presence into your birth space. Scripture tells us that "*faith comes by hearing, and hearing by the word of God*" (Romans 10:17 KJV). What better way to increase your faith, both your own and that of everyone in the room, than by reading, praying, and declaring the Word of God?

During my labors, I left my Bible open on my dresser to one of my favorite scriptures, alongside scripture cards I had created with verses I wanted to read if fear, anxiety, pain, or fatigue started to creep in. My husband would bring them to me, read them aloud, and we would pray together. Others can do this as well, such as your mother, doula, sister, or friend.

One of my favorite scriptures for prayer, protection, peace, and promise is Psalm 91. You can turn any scripture into a prayer or declaration. For example:

Father, I dwell in Your secret place under the shadow of the Almighty. You are my refuge and fortress, my God in whom I trust. You will surely deliver me from every snare and every deadly thing that would try to come against my baby or me. You cover me with Your feathers; under Your wings, I find refuge. Your faithfulness is my shield that surrounds this birth space, my body, and this child. I will not fear the pain of labor, the unknown, or the lies of the enemy. Terror will not come near me, day or night. Though a thousand may fall at my side and ten thousand at my right hand, it will not come near me. No harm will overtake me; no disaster will come near my dwelling. This birth space is covered by Your angels, whom You have commanded to guard me in all my ways. They will lift me up with their hands so that I do not stumble or fall. I will tread upon fear, doubt, and darkness because I carry Your name and walk in Your authority . Because I love You, You will rescue me. You will protect me, for I acknowledge Your name. When I call on You, You answer me. You are with me in trouble and will deliver me. You will honor me as Your daughter. With a long life, You will satisfy me and show me Your salvation in my body, in this birth, and in the life of my child. I receive Your promises with faith and surrender. I welcome Your holy presence into this sacred moment. In Jesus's name, amen.

Worship & Praise

Worshipping during labor is another wonderful way to invite the Lord's presence into this time and space. When we worship, we create room for God to dwell in the moment. According to Psalm 22:3, His presence brings peace, comfort, and power.

In the birth room, worship can transform a fearful space into a holy place where the spirit of God is tangibly felt. Worship is also a form of spiritual warfare; darkness, fear, and anxiety cannot remain where God is magnified. Scripture supports this idea. Worship sends confusion into the enemy's camp, as demonstrated in 2 Chronicles 20:21–22.

Praise serves as a weapon of vengeance against evil (Psalm 149:5–9). Praise and worship replace heaviness and fear (Isaiah 61:3). Labor can make us inwardly focused and overwhelmed; worship reorients us back to Jesus, the source of our strength, peace, and help. It reminds us that we are not alone and do not have to face this in our own might.

Worship music can also have a profound effect on us physiologically. It can calm the nervous system, slow breathing and heart rate, lower cortisol levels, and encourage the release of oxytocin, the hormone that promotes connection, peace, and labor progression.[1]

During the birth of my first child, my labor was not really changing, so my doula suggested that we turn on some music. I had prepared a worship birth playlist, and once I played it, I instantly started crying. This emotional release helped trigger the release of oxytocin, and within minutes, my labor shifted dramatically. Worship had a significant impact on my labor progression.

Physical Movement

Many spiritual factors influence us physically, as I've mentioned, and this is part of God's design. But what other physical steps can we take during labor to align ourselves with God?

God didn't just create our bodies; He engineered them with incredible precision. Here are some practices to consider:

Positioning

The same way the baby enters the birth canal is how they can be encouraged to exit. Different positions can help the baby descend. Some helpful positions aligned with God's design are hands-and-knees, squatting, upright standing or walking, side-lying, and lunging or step position.

---

1. Verena Wulff, Philip Hepp, Oliver T. Wolf, Percy Balan, Carsten Hagenbeck, Tanja Fehm, and Nora K. Schaal, "The Effects of a Music and Singing Intervention During Pregnancy on Maternal Well-Being and Mother-Infant Bonding: A Randomised, Controlled Study," *Archives of Gynecology and Obstetrics* 303, no. 1 (2021): 69–83, https://doi.org/10.1007/s00404-020-05727-8.

Touch

Techniques like hip squeezes can reduce muscle tension, provide reassurance, decrease anxiety, and enhance a woman's sense of control. Touch can also distract from pain, lower blood pressure, and ease labor. Hip squeezes help push the ilia together, relieving pressure on the sacroiliac joint.

Vocalization

The "sphincter law," a principle observed in natural birth, highlights how fearfully and wonderfully God made us. Sphincters are involuntary muscles surrounding the openings of various organs, such as the cervix and mouth.

God designed these muscles to stay closed for protection and to open only under the right conditions. They do not tire easily like voluntary muscles and respond to safety, privacy, warmth, and trust, rather than force or stress. This demonstrates God's wisdom in creating birth to be a cooperative event between spirit, mind, and body; it is not something to be muscled through but surrendered to.

God created the jaw, throat, and pelvic sphincters to be neurologically and hormonally connected. When your mouth is relaxed, your pelvic floor and cervix are more likely to open, whereas a tense jaw can create a tight cervix.

A relaxed jaw is linked to an open cervix. Deep, low moaning relaxes the throat and encourages the pelvis to soften. In contrast, high-pitched screaming can tighten the throat, disrupting the body's natural processes.

In most movie scenes depicting childbirth, you often see women screaming. However, this activates the sympathetic nervous system, triggering a fight-or-flight response. High-pitched screams, typically a response to fear, panic, or pain, trigger the release of adrenaline and cortisol.

This release can actually slow or stall contractions, as adrenaline counteracts oxytocin. Labor works best when a woman is in a calm, safe, and supportive environment; fear can disrupt this process and pull you out of your body's natural rhythm.

Labor relies on deep focus and instinctual movement. High-pitched screaming interrupts that flow, while deep, low sounds such as moaning and humming align better with the parasympathetic nervous system, helping the cervix to soften and open.

Screaming can create tension in the pelvic floor. It is often accompanied by a clenched jaw, tense shoulders, and a tightened pelvic floor, which can make it more difficult for the baby to descend. Relaxation and low vocal tones keep muscles soft and receptive.

You never have to feel shame or embarrassment if screaming feels instinctual during labor; this is something to just be aware of. Understand that the physiological responses your physical body will have are based on God's design for your body.

Breath Work

The way you position your body spiritually can significantly affect your physical state during labor, especially your breathing. There are various breathing techniques that can promote relaxation, allowing you to flow with your body's natural rhythms and follow its design.

Giving birth is a significant act of surrender, and breathing, rather than resisting, is the most effective way to work with your body's design. Several breathing techniques can align with this design based on the stage of labor you are in.

In early labor, the uterus begins to contract rhythmically, thinning or effacing the cervix and opening it. Contractions during this phase may be mild to moderate, lasting thirty to forty-five seconds and spaced fifteen to twenty minutes apart. During this time, deep, open-mouth breathing can be very effective. Inhaling deeply through the nose, expanding the belly, and then exhaling slowly through the mouth as if gently blowing out a candle keeps oxygen flowing to both mother and baby, slows the heart rate, and prevents unnecessary tension in the pelvic floor. Relaxed muscles allow the uterus to function efficiently without resistance.

In the next stage, active labor, rhythmic breathing, and deep vocalization can be helpful. Contractions become stronger and longer, lasting between forty-five and sixty seconds and occurring every three to five minutes. The uterus works harder, increasing intrauterine pressure to continue dilating the cervix.

At this stage, the pelvic floor begins to release and open naturally, but tension can impede progress if you hold your breath or tense up. Rhythmic breathing, combined with deep vocalization, helps maintain a steady oxygen supply and promotes relaxation. For example, breathing in through your nose for a count of four and then out through your mouth for a count of six, whatever feels comfortable, can be effective. This technique helps you stay focused and calm, reducing feelings of panic and overwhelm.

During the transition phase, contractions peak in intensity, lasting sixty to ninety seconds, with only thirty seconds to two minutes of rest in between. The uterus is almost fully dilated, and the baby is descending lower into the birth canal, putting significant pressure on the cervix and pelvic floor. Many women feel the urge to push before the cervix is fully ready, which can necessitate breathing through contractions instead of pushing down.

Growl breathing, also known as he-he breathing, can be highly beneficial during transition. This technique involves making deep, rhythmic growls. Begin by taking two to three quick breaths or growls, followed by a longer one. This approach allows you to relax into the intensity of contractions, releasing tension through vocalization rather than fighting against it.

Using this method helps prevent you from pushing too soon, reduces tension in the pelvic floor, and ensures a steady flow of oxygen. It also helps manage feelings of being overwhelmed by rapid contractions.

During the final stage of labor, the pushing stage, when you are ten centimeters dilated, the cervix is fully open. The uterus will involuntarily contract to push the baby down. It's essential for the pelvic floor muscles to stretch and fully release, while coordinated pushing helps guide the baby through the birth canal. Panting can be particularly effective in this phase.

Practice taking two to three quick, shallow breaths or pants, followed by a longer breath. This technique prevents you from pushing too forcefully, decreases pelvic floor tension, and maintains oxygen flow during intense contractions.

Another valuable technique is J-breathing. Inhale deeply through your nose, then exhale through your mouth while gently bearing down, directing your breath and pressure downward as if blowing air through a straw or creating a J-shape with your breath going down and out. This method aligns with the body's natural fetal ejection reflex, reducing the risk of tearing by keeping the perineum relaxed and minimizing exhaustion compared to traditional coached or purple pushing.

In addition to specific breathing techniques, prayer breathing offers a profound way to focus on your breath during labor. Remember that each breath you take is a gift from a powerful, omnipresent God. Genesis 2:7 (NLT) states, *"Then the LORD God formed the man from the dust of the ground. He breathed the breath of life into the man's nostrils, and the man became a living person."* Each breath you take reflects His gift of life, strength, and power.

As you breathe, remember that it is His breath in your lungs and that He is with you. To keep your focus on Jesus throughout labor, meditate on these scriptures and pray as you breathe through each contraction:

Inhale: "I will not be afraid."
Exhale: "For you are with me" (Psalm 91).

Inhale: "The Lord is my refuge."

Exhale: "Nothing can harm me" (1 Peter 5:7).

Inhale: "I give you my worries."
Exhale: "For you care about me" (Romans 8:38–39).

Inhale: "Nothing can separate me."
Exhale: "From your love."

Water

Another practical tip for labor is the use of water, which holds significant spiritual meaning. Water is mentioned in the Bible 722 times, more often than faith, hope, prayer, and worship. It was created on the very first day by God (Genesis 1:2). Water flows throughout scripture, reminding us of its importance both spiritually and physically.

Water symbolizes the Holy Spirit's ability to refresh us, quench our spiritual thirst, cleanse us, and bring forth life wherever He flows. It has the power to heal, as seen in the story of Naaman, who was cured of leprosy in the waters of the Jordan (2 Kings 5:1–14). Water purifies and provides deliverance.

Using water during labor can help you relax, reduce cortisol levels, and increase oxytocin, which may alleviate pain.[2] Remember the benefits of water therapy for pain management, but also allow it to remind you that the Holy Spirit flows through you, refreshing and strengthening you, bringing forth life.

---

2. Rebecca D. Benfield, Tibor Hortobágyi, Charles J. Tanner, Melvin Swanson, Margaret M. Heitkemper, and Edward R. Newton, "The Effects of Hydrotherapy on Anxiety, Pain, Neuroendocrine Responses, and Contraction Dynamics During Labor," *Biological Research for Nursing* **12, no. 1** (2010): 28–36, https://doi.org/10.1177/1099800410361535.

The Husband

Lastly, I want to share the role the husband can play during labor, one that aligns with the biblical role God created for man.

In scripture, we see man's role as a protector, guarding his wife's physical, emotional, and spiritual environment; a provider, ensuring she has what she needs to thrive; a priest, leading her spiritually, praying for her, and bringing her into God's presence; and a partner, standing beside her as one flesh, not above her.

On the other hand, God called women a *"helper suitable"* (Genesis 2:18 NIV), which is not a lesser role but one that mirrors the Holy Spirit's nature: comforter, nurturer, and life-giver. Women are designed to receive and bring forth life. Our power flows through surrender, peace, and connection.

When considering birth, it's important to recognize the distinct roles each person plays. The mother is the one giving birth, while the husband is meant to be a protector. God designed women to be soft, which is often the opposite of what the world preaches about birth (again, something we have to muster and power through in our own strength).

Culturally, there is often a perception that during labor, the focus is mainly on the mother, with the medical team attending to her while the father is relegated to the sidelines. However, based on God's design, we are missing out by not having an actively participating husband.

My personal experiences have been very different. I wanted my husband to be actively involved because, in our relationship, he is the leader of our home and my protector. I saw him as my rock physically, emotionally, and spiritually during labor.

To prepare him for this role, I made it a priority to pray that he would feel confident and spiritually equipped. I also invited him to learn about God's design for labor, which helped him understand how to support me physically, mentally, and spiritually through the process.

The presence of a father figure during labor is incredibly important, as he can be a strong source of support. My husband embodied this perfectly. When he began reading scripture over me, the atmosphere in the room changed. I felt a profound sense of peace and was able to refocus on trusting God throughout the process, rather than dwelling on my emotional or physical discomforts. I was able to remain soft and receptive.

GOD'S DESIGN, HIS STRENGTH, YOUR BIRTH

You are designed to labor and give birth to your baby. God will not leave you unprepared; He is equipping you right now, not just physically but also spiritually, mentally, and emotionally. Throughout scripture, we see themes and tools that God provided to help His people endure, overcome, and navigate trials with peace, power, and purpose. These same tools apply to childbirth.

The Bible isn't just a collection of stories; it's a guide for our lives and a source of coping mechanisms and life-giving power. It is a supernatural book giving you supernatural abilities. By inviting the Holy Spirit into every aspect of labor and walking by His Spirit, you will not have to rely on your own strength, but rather can tap into the same power that raised Jesus from the grave, aligning yourself with His design rather than working against it.

QUESTIONS FOR REFLECTION

Before the day arrives, here are some questions to consider:

1. Do I trust in God's design for my body and His timing for my labor and delivery, or am I leaning more on medical interventions or worldly systems because of fear?
2. Have I spoken words of fear, doubt, or negativity over my birth experience, or am I declaring God's truth and promises?

3. Am I harboring unforgiveness, bitterness, or resentment that could give the enemy a foothold in my heart or home?
4. Have I prayed over my birth and my birth team, including doctors, nurses, midwives, and doulas, inviting the Holy Spirit to guide their actions and decisions?
5. Do I seek God as my ultimate source of peace, or am I relying on external tools, techniques, or people to calm my anxiety?
6. Have I asked the Holy Spirit to reveal any lies I may have believed about childbirth that stem from fear rather than faith?
7. Am I consistently praying for and speaking blessings over my baby's birth, or am I allowing fear or doubt to creep into my mind?
8. Have I protected my mind from negative birth stories, fear-based advice, or media that contradicts God's word?

7

GOD, DID YOU HEAR ME?

In the previous chapters, I explained God's heart for women, particularly regarding pregnancy and childbirth. I discussed how the fall of humanity introduced sin into the world, affecting the entire reproductive process. Living in this fallen world means we may face hardship and experience pain. There might be times when we feel confused, wondering where God is amid our situations.

Pregnancy and childbirth are humbling experiences. While our flesh desires to control everything, ultimately, we cannot. If you have learned anything from this book so far, or more importantly, if your mindset has shifted in any way during your reading, I pray that you can see that God invites you to surrender this process to Him. This surrender means not trying to control everything, but rather partnering with Him, gaining wisdom, being refined, walking by His spirit, and stepping into the motherhood experience He has for you.

I now want to take time to walk through a common question many women have regarding their childbirth experiences: "God, did you hear me?" I want to confirm one thing with certainty: God always hears your prayers (1 John 5:14–15). God is not distant and will respond immediately; however, in this fallen world, it's also important to understand that there are real demonic powers and principalities trying to block our prayers, oppress God's people, and inflict pain on them.

In Daniel 10:12-13 we see this clearly. *"Then he said, 'Don't be afraid, Daniel. Since the first day you began to pray for understanding and to humble yourself before your God, your request has been heard in heaven. I have come in answer to your prayer. But for twenty-one days the spirit prince of the kingdom of Persia blocked my way. Then Michael, one of the archangels, came to help me, and I left him there with the spirit prince of the kingdom of Persia."*

Daniel prayed, and heaven responded immediately; however, the "prince," which was a territorial demonic principality, resisted in the spirit realm. I believe there is a misconception among many that believe if your prayer isn't being answered, it must be because God didn't hear it; however, the Bible tells us otherwise and makes a strong case for believers to exercise their authority through the name of Jesus to come against these powers of darkness.

Additionally, there actually are some hindrances to prayer that we see in Scripture. These hindrances include: praying out of our own selfish ambition (James 4:3), unconfessed or hidden sin (Isaiah 59:1-2), idols in your heart (Ezekiel 14:3), stinginess and the lack of liberality toward the poor and God's work (Proverbs 21:13), unforgiveness as prayer is answered on the basis that our sins are forgiven (Mark 11:25), wrong relation between man and wife (1 Peter 3:7), and lastly, by unbelief (James 1:5-7).

As someone who believes in the amazing power of prayer and how very important it is to include prayer in our everyday lives and walk with Christ, especially during pregnancy leading up to the birth of our babies, it's important to have an understanding of what scripture says about answered prayers instead of just how we feel (and our feelings are often far from the truth).

THE BALANCE OF AUTHORITY AND SURRENDER

The experience of childbirth is meant to be a blessing, not a burden. God is for you, not against you. But what do you do when you do all the right things, yet your plans still don't unfold as expected? Let's say you really tap into God's presence. You go to Him for wisdom. You tear down your idols. You speak with authority over your baby's birth, declaring the Word of God.

You physically prepare to work with God's design, not against it, and attach actions to your faith. You worship and praise, and then your birth doesn't go as you envisioned. This situation raises the question: what happened? Is there a line when it comes to standing in authority over our baby's birth, declaring the Word, and believing God for the desires of our hearts, paired with a humble surrender?

Matthew 7:7 says, "Ask, and you shall receive," right? But is there a line? The scriptures clearly instruct us to stand in our God-given authority, speaking the Word, declaring God's promises, and aligning with Heaven's will. These are powerful acts of faith, and we must do these things.

We see this concept throughout scripture.

"Look, I have given you authority over all the power of the enemy, and you can walk among snakes and scorpions and crush them. Nothing will injure you."(Luke 10:19 NLT). *"You will also decree a thing, and it will be established for you"* (Job 22:28 NASB). *"Death and life are in the power of the tongue"* (Proverbs 18:21 NKJV).

There is power in speaking in faith. If you have positive expectancy, believe, and know that God's Word will come to pass, you will be rewarded. It is important to truly believe that when Jesus died for you, He gave you authority and His Word, and that it will come to pass. Hebrews 11:6 (NLT) even tells us, *"And it is impossible to please God without faith. Anyone who wants to come to Him must believe that God exists and that He rewards those who sincerely seek Him."*

However, it's crucial to understand that faith is not control. There is a fine line between faith and control. Sometimes, without realizing it, we approach God like a vending machine: insert prayer, declaration, and worship, and out comes the birth we envisioned. But God is not a formula; He is a Father and desires our relationship, not performance.

Declaring God's word should not merely be transactional; it has to be spoken with faith attached to it. However, biblical faith is not about manipulating outcomes; it's about trusting the One who holds those outcomes, believing even when we can't see, and acting on our faith. Hebrews 11:1 (AMPC), "*NOW FAITH is the assurance (the confirmation, the title deed) of the things we hope for, being the proof of things we do not see and the conviction of their reality—faith perceiving as real fact what is not revealed to the senses.*"

Pregnancy and birth are deeply physical, emotional, and spiritual experiences. They challenge us to confront both our vulnerabilities and our hope. When we zoom out, we can see that our surrender and putting our faith in God is not merely about getting through labor; it's about being shaped more fully into the image of Christ and the spirit-filled mother He has called you to be. Jesus's life demonstrates the Kingdom's pattern: surrender leads to glory, not worldly glory, but the kind that transforms the soul and reveals God's love and presence in the most unexpected places.

In the same way, your pregnancy and birth, even if they don't unfold according to the plan that you envisioned, can become sacred ground for transformation. Any deviation from what you prayed for is not wasted in the hands of God. We must remember that God is a good God, and the devil is a bad devil. If something occurs during childbirth that causes distress, fear, or trauma, this is not God! He doesn't cause pain (and I'm not talking about the sensations that accompany childbirth, there is purpose to sensation in childbirth, and it is not punishment), but God does use anything bad for our good. He doesn't waste tears, but He does use them (Psalm 126:5, NLT).

Our actions, prayers, and declarations should align us with Him, not seek to control Him. Scriptural declarations do not force God's hand; they align our hearts with His. They speak truth into the atmosphere, remind us of His promises, and strengthen us. Jesus tells us, "*I tell you the truth, whatever you forbid on earth will be forbidden in heaven, and whatever you permit on earth will be permitted in heaven.*" (Matthew 18:18, NLT). Heaven supports the God-aligned authority exercised on earth. This is about spiritual authority and agreement with God's will. It's not us commanding heaven; it's heaven enforcing what's already God's will when we pray in alignment.

But how will we know what the will of the Father is? We know the will of the Father by reading and studying His word. Putting it together biblically can look like:

- Asking in Jesus's name = asking in alignment with His character, authority, and purposes
- According to His will = in agreement with His word and nature
- Abiding in Him = staying rooted in truth, not how we feel

In preparation to give birth, I made declarations like, "My birth will be peaceful, protected, and filled with joy." But how could I be sure that was God's will for me? I know God's will for me is to have peace and joy. When scripture says, "*Surely your goodness and unfailing love will pursue me all the days of my life*" (Psalm 23:6), this does not exclude the day I give birth. Take scripture and make it personal!

I prayed many things before I gave birth. I prayed, "Lord, help me hear Your Holy Spirit clearly to guide every breath and movement. Let my husband and me be unified during this process. Help me surrender fully to the process You created. Help me rest and not resist, allowing my body to flow with the rhythm You established. Let me birth in joy, not just without pain, but with laughter and praise.

Let me feel heaven in the room, experiencing Your tangible presence."

I prayed that my birth would prophesy God's goodness, grace, and power. After I had my first baby, I remember asking God why I felt pain when my son was being born. I prayed and believed, so why did I feel pain? I remember hearing, *"It's because you didn't fully believe it was possible. You didn't believe hard enough."*

While faith is essential when it comes to our prayers (James 1:6–7), I believe this is a whisper in the ears of many believers who are trusting the Lord with their births. When things don't go exactly as we hope, Satan uses that as an opportunity to make us question God and His love for us, twisting the truth, sowing doubt, and challenging our understanding of God's goodness.

This tactic is not new; it began in the Garden of Eden. In Genesis 3:1–5 (NIV), the serpent asked Eve, *"Did God really say you must not eat from any tree in the garden?"* He then said, *"You will not certainly die,"* and implied that God was withholding something from them. This was the first act of spiritual deception.

The enemy didn't directly attack God; instead, he planted doubt in Eve's mind about God's Word and His goodness. This is the same tactic used against us: did God really say your birth would be enjoyable? If God truly loved you, wouldn't He have answered your prayers exactly as you requested?

Satan causes us to question God's word and, ultimately, His character. In Matthew 4:3 (NIV), during the temptation of Jesus, the tempter questioned His identity and relationship with the Father, saying, *"If you are the Son of God..."* He was implying that if Jesus was genuinely loved by God, why was He suffering? Why wasn't God showing up the way He wanted?

It's the same voice that questions a mother after giving birth: if you truly had faith and authority, then why did it hurt? Why did it go the way it did? Why did it end up in a C-section, the one thing you didn't want? But Jesus didn't take Satan's bait; He responded with the truth, the Word.

In Job 1:2, we see Job being tested. Satan tells God that Job only loves Him because of His blessings. Then Job loses nearly everything, and his friends imply that he must have done something wrong. This reflects a common theme: if things didn't go as you wanted, you must have failed. However, Job had done nothing wrong. His suffering was not proof of God's absence or a lack of faith.

Instead, it became a backdrop for deeper revelation and intimacy with God. In Revelation 12:10 (NLT), scripture describes Satan as the accuser: *"For the accuser of our brothers and sisters, who accuses them before our God day and night, has been thrown down."*

That accusing voice tells you that you didn't believe hard enough, that you didn't do it right, and that you must have disappointed God. That is not the voice of God; that is the voice of the accuser. Faith is also not something you try harder to obtain; it comes from hearing the word of God (Romans 10:17). Faith lives in the spirit, not just the intellect. Hearing the Word allows the Spirit to reveal truth internally, which is completely supernatural. If faith were something we achieved, it would be a work, and scripture consistently separates faith from works. If you want to build your faith, you immerse yourself in the Word; you don't "try harder" to believe (read that a few more times until it sinks in).

While Satan would love for you to focus on what didn't happen or what went wrong, blaming yourself for a lack of faith, we must push past guilt and condemnation as believers and keep our eyes on Jesus. We must use Job as an example. Our circumstances and feelings are real, but they do not change who Jesus is, what He did for us, and the power and authority His Word carries.

YOUR DESIRES ARE NEVER IN VAIN

We live in a culture where, when things don't go as expected, we are led to believe it's not a big deal. What I want you to understand is that anything related to your pregnancy or childbirth experience is significant. If things don't go the way you hoped, it doesn't mean something is wrong or that God wasn't present. Before you read any further, I want you to continue to have positive expectations of these experiences. Just because unfavorable outcomes can happen does not mean they will.

You still have the right to grieve the loss of the experience you wanted, whether it was big or small. All of it matters to God. Feeling sad, disappointed, or even angry if your birth experience doesn't go as you planned is entirely normal, especially when you prepared so well.

I've spoken to countless women who carry hidden grief, often silently, because they believe it shouldn't matter since their baby is healthy. This is a lie from the enemy. A loss is a loss, and it absolutely matters to God.

I talk to women almost daily who have dealt with disappointments around childbirth, big and small, and it has led me to seek God's heart in these "Why, God?" situations. What I've realized is that as followers of Jesus, we are not immune to grief. Your grief doesn't make you weak; it doesn't mean you didn't have enough faith.

More faith isn't always the solution because grief isn't a spiritual failure; it's simply a part of being human. It's even part of being like Jesus, as He experienced grief as well.

Here's what unaddressed grief around childbirth can look like:

1. **Denial:** "I'm fine. My baby's fine." But underneath, there's bitterness.
2. **Discounting:** "It's not that big of a deal what happened during my baby's birth." In reality, however, it was significant.
3. **Numbing:** We distract ourselves and miss God's comfort.
4. **Disqualification:** "Other women have had it worse, so I shouldn't feel this way."

If you never unpack the grief from what you went through, you'll feel disconnected from others, from yourself, and even from God. It can manifest in motherhood as bitterness, resentment, and anger.

But here's the hope: God is in the process of allowing you to feel what happened. He's in the community that surrounds you, saying, *"It happened to me, too."*

We often view grief as negative, but it's a godly experience because even Jesus grieved. Because of His resurrection, we have a new way to process our pain with hope. Never assume that God cannot work something good out of your story. Don't try to skip the season or miss out on what He has for you.

And don't believe the lie from the enemy that your preparation was in vain. God honors wisdom and invites you to prepare. Part of God's design for birth is our faith, and with our faith is our preparation that is attached to it.

He loves it when we care for our bodies and our births with intention. However, the enemy often twists wisdom into control, suggesting that if we had just done a little more, perhaps things would have turned out differently. However, the truth is that wisdom is not the same as control. Preparation does not guarantee a specific result. Faithful preparation is never wasted. All your preparation for childbirth is an act of worship and faith unto the Lord.

The enemy will try to make you believe that you have failed, making you hesitant to try again. But God sees your heart and continues to write your story, and it's a good one! We know that for those who love God, for those who are called according to His purpose, all things work together for good (Romans 8:28). So, continue to prepare, plan, and pray boldly for the birth you desire. You are going to accept God's invitation to follow His design for childbirth and be filled with praise!

FROM LABOR TO LIFE: A GLIMPSE OF THE GOSPEL

At this point, you can see that birth is not just a physical event; it is a spiritual invitation. What you may not yet fully understand, and what I want to highlight, is that childbirth offers a glimpse into the gospel itself: from discomfort to delivery, from labor to life, and from surrender to new creation. When we focus solely on the desired outcome, we risk missing the invitation to know God more deeply, to become more like Christ, and to trust that even if we don't understand, He is working for our good and His glory. As Isaiah 55:9 (NLT) says, *"For just as the heavens are higher than the earth, so my ways are higher than your ways, and my thoughts higher than your thoughts."*

When you surrender your birth to God, you're not giving up or saying, "Whatever happens, happens"; you are diligently following His design and entrusting it to the One who writes the best stories. Sometimes, God delivers us from hardship, and sometimes, He walks us through it. Both are expressions of His love and reveal His glory.

I've come to realize that when we ask, "Why, God?" the answer reflects the complexities of motherhood. Just as we don't always explain our decisions to our children, not out of cruelty, but because they can't grasp the larger picture, so too may God withhold the answers, not out of distance but out of love. His ways may not always align with ours, but His heart is always good.

Following God's design during childbirth is just one part of God's invitation to us to draw closer. The realization that I cannot control my circumstances, but understanding that Jesus is constant, led me beautifully into motherhood. I will share this experience in detail in the next section of this book.

QUESTIONS FOR REFLECTION

1. When I pray and declare God's Word over my life, do I trust Him enough to accept outcomes I cannot control?
2. In what areas do I need to practice more surrender while still standing boldly in faith over my circumstances?

PART 3

CARRYING THE FIRE FORWARD

Father God, thank You for this sacred and holy journey that this mother has walked with You.
As she reads these final pages, I pray that Your Holy Spirit ignites a fire within her, a fire that burns not from striving, but from surrender; not from fear, but from faith. Let her carry the flame of Your presence into every room she enters. May her mothering be marked by heaven, not by the world's expectations but by Your design.
Grant her the courage to raise her children in truth, to disciple them in love, and to remain deeply rooted in Your Word. Lord, may she never forget that You chose her for this, not just to carry life in her womb but to carry Your glory into the next generation. Let the fire burn bright and never go out.
In Jesus's mighty name, amen.

8

KEEP YOUR FLAME BURNING

Once you hold your baby in your arms, you officially enter a new season: postpartum. This season can be overwhelming, and it's easy to lose sight of the mission you were on in the first place: the holy invitation you accepted during pregnancy and the birth of your baby to grow in intimacy with the Lord, surrender control, be refined, pray without ceasing, walk by His spirit, and prepare for Kingdom motherhood. All of this is not just about having a baby but about becoming the mother God designed you to be.

This is about your calling. Pregnancy and birth are God's invitation to partner with Him in raising disciples and to grow His Kingdom. Now, you've begun this journey. You've walked through pregnancy. You've labored, birthed, and surrendered. You've welcomed life into the world, but instead of basking in joy and peace, you may find yourself in a fog, confused, exhausted, anxious, and perhaps even numb. This isn't always just due to hormones or a lack of sleep. Yes, there are physical and emotional changes, but a spiritual battle is unfolding as well.

The enemy knows what's at stake in your postpartum season: your identity, your confidence, your connection with God, and the generational legacy you are building. He despises what you've just accomplished, partnering with God to bring forth life, and he will try to undermine everything sacred about your new role as a mother. Just as Jesus was tempted in the wilderness after His spiritual high point at baptism (Luke 4), many women experience spiritual resistance right after the miracle of birth. This is not random; it's strategic. The enemy waits until we are vulnerable, tired, and overwhelmed to strike.

But you don't have to face this battle alone. You move forward from a place of victory because Jesus already defeated the devil. Victory, not defeat, is your inheritance in Christ! You can recognize the enemy's schemes, put on the Armor of God (Ephesians 6:10–18), respond with the Word, and invite the Holy Spirit to continue refining you during this season, rather than letting it destroy you.

FROM STRUGGLE TO SPIRITUAL BREAKTHROUGH

When I was postpartum with my first baby, before I had an encounter with Jesus and fully surrendered my life to Him, I experienced immense spiritual warfare without realizing what was happening. Because I hadn't surrendered to Jesus, I also caved to my flesh and my thoughts; I didn't know how to take them captive. Struggling with our flesh and minds is another battle we face, but I thought this was just normal hormonal turmoil, a part of postpartum life as the world describes it, just like pregnancy and birth.

After a few months, as the initial postpartum haze began to lift, I started exercising and felt more like myself. But then I quickly became obsessed with my body image. I had an image in my mind of how my body used to look, and I wanted to regain that. I placed my self-worth and identity on how I looked and struggled with feelings of comparison and pride regarding my body image.

I didn't want people to look at me and think, *Oh, she just had a baby*, but rather, *Wow, she looks really good.* I sought validation from others. While this may seem like typical postpartum behavior, I want to emphasize that it isn't always just that. My thoughts consumed me to the point where preparing to go out, whether to see friends or family, became a lengthy ordeal. I would spend forever searching for the perfect outfit that made me feel acceptable. If I didn't look or feel a certain way, I would spiral into anxiety.

This was the first attack on my identity postpartum. As time went on, I began to feel a strong desire to have another baby. This is where my obsession with fitness transformed into an obsession with becoming pregnant again, something else I could attempt to control.

I made sure to do all the right things: taking my supplements and tracking my cycle perfectly. It was during this time of wanting another baby that I met the Lord. Almost every thought I had was about when I would become pregnant again.

However, on the day I encountered Jesus and truly felt the love of God for the first time, the veil was lifted from my eyes. In that moment, I realized I was placing my identity in the gift of motherhood, rather than in the giver, Christ. I had made pregnancy and the idea of motherhood an idol. Both are good, but I allowed them to define me more than Christ did. I recognized that I had been in a battle for my identity, and I was losing, not because I wasn't fighting hard enough, but because I was fighting in my own strength instead of surrendering.

The moment I repented, released my burdens, and went to the feet of Jesus was when true peace entered my life. He didn't fix everything immediately, but He re-centered me, and that was the real healing I needed.

Suddenly, I realized I had stopped looking at myself in the mirror constantly. I no longer cared about what I was going to wear, and I could get ready without comparing myself to others or worrying about how they would perceive me. Most importantly, I found an instant cessation of my longing for another baby.

My perspective shifted completely, and I became much more aware and discerning over time. After I had my second baby, I could see the spiritual battle around me. Although my postpartum experience was significantly different and I walked with Jesus during this time, it didn't mean I was immune to attacks from the enemy.

SEEING THE BATTLE CLEARLY

In this next section, I want to share the tactics used to negatively influence us. However, before I move on, I want to reiterate that not everything comes from the enemy. In a broken world, we still have to resist our flesh and the sinful nature it desires as a result of the fall, as well as break strongholds (or what I like to call habits, some that get passed down generationally).

Postpartum is a vulnerable season marked by many physical and emotional changes, and while you deserve grace in this season, it's still a time to be aware of the temptations of our flesh and the bad habits we have, not to condemn or fall into mom-guilt but to resist them.

Looking at scripture and seeing themes of how people were influenced negatively in vulnerable times also helps me be aware of the enemy's schemes, as well as where I might be vulnerable in general.

As you read through these, read them through a lens of victory, not of defeat. Just because there is a potential for challenging times while we are in this fallen world, does not mean that we have to accept or agree with them. You are victorious through Jesus Christ!

Here are some examples you can reflect on and be aware of:

Doubt (Genesis 3:1)

The enemy questions God's promises, your worth, and your abilities. You might hear things like, *Did God really call you to be a mother? You're not naturally maternal like other moms. Are you sure God is listening to your prayers? You've been crying out and still feel anxious.* You might even think, *Maybe I misunderstood when God said that this baby was a blessing. This doesn't feel like a blessing.*

Disbelief (Matthew 13:58)

Doubt can deepen into unbelief; you may think that God will never move or help you. You might hear thoughts like, *I've prayed for peace, but I still feel chaotic. Maybe this is just how it's going to be.* You may feel: *God's not going to heal this postpartum depression. It's too far gone. I'm never going to sleep again. This is just my new reality. God might perform miracles for others, but not for me.*

Distraction (Luke 10:40)

The enemy uses busyness, noise, and mental clutter to keep you from focusing on God. You might think, *I'll read my Bible after I get the baby down, or maybe tomorrow. There's no time for worship. I have diapers, dishes, and zero time for myself.* Mindless scrolling can replace moments of stillness or hearing from God, and you might feel, *I'm too exhausted to pray. God understands.*

Discouragement (Numbers 13:31–33)

The enemy whispers that you're failing, unseen, and not enough. You may hear thoughts like, *You're a terrible mom for snapping when you were tired. You're not bonding with your baby the way you should.* You might compare yourself to others, thinking, *Look at that mom on Instagram. Why can't you get it together? Everyone else makes this look easy.*

Disappointment (Ruth 1:20)

We are not immune to disappointment, and we see in scripture that there can be real times of feeling let down. It's okay to feel, but be aware of your thoughts. *What's wrong with me? I feel disappointment. My expectations for postpartum life feel shattered. I thought I would experience instant joy, but instead, I feel overwhelmed and distant. I imagined my husband would be more supportive and sensitive. Breastfeeding was supposed to come naturally, so why is it so painful? I expected to bounce back physically, but I don't recognize myself anymore.* You might feel a theme of disappointment, but this leaves the door open to God's restorative power.

Delay (Genesis 16:1–2)

When healing, peace, or restoration doesn't come quickly, it's easy to feel tempted to give up. *Why do I still not feel like myself after six weeks? I thought I would be back at church or engaged in my community by now. I've been praying for joy for months, but maybe it's just not coming. My hormones feel out of control, and I worry that this might be permanent.*

Deception (2 Corinthians 11:14)

Blessings can be disguised as burdens, and pressure to take care of everything on your own or carry all of the weight feels required. *I should handle everything on my own now that I'm a mom. I need to be strong, and needing help is a sign of weakness. Self-care is selfish; I should be focusing entirely on my baby. Maybe God is punishing me for something, and that's why this is all so hard.*

Division (1 Corinthians 1:10–13)

A sense of division creeps in, creating disunity in relationships. *My husband doesn't understand me anymore, and I resent him for it. He doesn't check on me, so I start to think that maybe no one really cares. I even feel disconnected from God.*

Defeat (1 Kings 19:4)

You're led to believe this season has beaten you. *I worry I'll never recover emotionally from this birth experience. I feel like I have lost who I was and that I'll never get her back. I don't feel like a joyful person anymore; motherhood feels like it has broken me.*

Depression/Despair (Psalm 143:3–4)

The enemy preys on physical and emotional exhaustion in the postpartum period, making it easier to spiral into hopelessness, and the Bible tells us that heaviness is a spirit (Isaiah 61:3). *I feel like I can't go on anymore. I just want to escape. Sometimes I think my baby might be better off with someone else. What's the point of getting up today? I find myself crying every day, and I don't see this getting any better.*

Disobedience (James 1:14–15)

We can fall into disobedience as a temptation from Satan but also from our own flesh. *I feel too tired to forgive or to speak kindly. I'm justified in snapping at others. I think God understands if I skip church, small group, or prayer time indefinitely. This is just survival mode. I'll return to God later.*

Destruction (John 10:10)

All these tactics aim to tear apart your peace, your family, your calling, and your faith. *I worry I'll never be emotionally whole again, that this season will ruin my marriage, and that I'm not the mom my baby needs. I struggle with the belief that God won't restore what has been lost.*

I experienced every one of these to some degree, but I wanted to share one that I am very grateful I became aware of right out of the gate of becoming a mother. This is the division between husband and wife.

Biblically, marriage is not just a personal relationship; it's a spiritual covenant that reflects Christ and the Church. A strong, united marriage honors God and demonstrates His love to the world. If the foundation of the marriage can be affected, the children can be affected as well. Division in marriage can disrupt God's plans and generational blessings, but a harmonious marriage reflects God's kingdom on earth. When a husband and wife are united in faith and purpose, they are spiritually strong (Ecclesiastes 4:12).

In the early days of parenthood, my husband and I often had misunderstandings, not necessarily arguments but moments when our different perspectives on parenting clashed. Men and women approach things differently, and that was evident in how we dealt with parenting.

For example, when I would turn to my husband for comfort and share my emotions, he often responded with logical solutions, like suggesting we create a better schedule. While I appreciated his intention, it made me feel like I wasn't being a good-enough mother. These cycles of misunderstanding would occur frequently. It started to become evident that this was the enemy trying to foster a divisive atmosphere in our home, and we began putting our foot down, telling the devil that our house would serve the Lord.

In contrast, during my second postpartum journey, I was much more aware of these dynamics. Recognizing this helped my husband and me combat it more effectively, which isn't always easy.

In those challenging moments, our instinct might be to push away from each other and think, *You don't understand me!* This tendency toward division can be powerful. Instead, we chose to pray together, forgive quickly and easily, practice humility, and command any prideful spirits, such as Leviathan (as seen in Job 41), to leave our atmosphere in Jesus's name. As new creations in Christ, we began to understand our true identity and authority in Him, and the more we resisted the devil, the more he had to flee (James 4:7).

Again, there are many ways mothers can be attacked once they enter this postpartum season, but another one I want to highlight is one of the biggest lies ingrained in society: the idea of losing yourself after having a baby. This idolatry of identity is one of the most common and painful fears in motherhood, especially after giving birth. Combined with the lack of sleep and the changes in your body, it can feel overwhelming.

Your mind may feel foggy, and your dreams seem distant; time no longer feels like your own. The enemy wants you to grieve your old identity and to idolize it in a way that keeps you stuck, preventing you from surrendering to God's plan for your life. I've been there.

There is a significant spiritual influence behind this lie, so much so that women want to have kids less and less. The U.S. fertility rate has actually reached historic lows. In 2024, the rate fell to approximately 1.6 children per woman, below the replacement level of 2.1, indicating that the population is not reproducing at a rate sufficient to maintain its size.[1] Many have been deceived into thinking that having a baby will cause them to lose their identity when, in reality, motherhood is meant to change and refine you, not erase you.

There were times when I missed the old version of myself. I thought, *I don't recognize myself anymore. All I do is nurse the baby, change diapers, and survive. I miss when I could just do whatever I wanted whenever I wanted.*

It's normal to have these thoughts. However, I discovered that there's a fine line between reminiscing about the past and idolizing it. God showed me that my identity is not found in what I do but in Christ, who lives in me.

In Matthew 16, Jesus talks about losing your life and states that whoever loses their life for Him will actually find it. I deeply appreciate this scripture and its application to motherhood because motherhood doesn't erase your identity; it refines and sanctifies it.

---

1. "US Fertility Rate Drops to a New Low, CDC Data Finds," *Al Jazeera*, July 24, 2025, https://www.aljazeera.com/news/2025/7/24/us-fertility-rate-drops-to-a-new-low-cdc-data-finds.

In that refining process, you discover the woman and mother God intended you to be. When Jesus says you must lose your life to follow Him, He is not speaking of destruction; He is referring to a holy and positive transformation.

He extends a holy invitation to die to the old self so that something greater can rise. Motherhood can be part of that transformation. You don't lose versions of yourself; you lose your schedule, preferences, physical comfort, and tidy plans.

But in that loss and surrender, you don't disappear; you are found. It's not the loss of identity; it's the refining of it. No matter what the circumstances are, no matter how you feel, you will still be who God says you are: blessed coming in and going out (Deuteronomy 28:6), forgiven and redeemed, washed clean by the blood of Jesus (Ephesians 1:7), and more than a conqueror empowered to overcome through Christ (Romans 8:37).

Postpartum becomes a sacred season where the old self is shed, and the new self is born, the one God always saw. Let's not forget that this is precisely what Jesus modeled; He laid down His life to bring about resurrection, and that's what we get to model and carry as mothers daily.

As you allow God to change you during the postpartum season, you will discover your identity in Christ even more. It's essential to clarify what identity in Christ is not. It's not pretending you're okay all the time. It's not ignoring the grief of change or faking joy while you're still healing. It's about letting God define you by what He accomplished on the cross, rather than by your productivity, accomplishments, or past experiences.

Our childbirth experiences significantly impact the beginning of our motherhood journey. It's easy to tie your identity to how your birth went: *I'm a mom who failed to have a natural birth and had a C-section instead,* or *I'm a mom who gives birth at home.* This is not your identity. As this book explains, giving birth is important for many reasons, but it doesn't define you as a mother.

Your identity in Christ is about letting love, not fear, be your foundation. Here's what God says about your identity: You are chosen (1 Peter 2:9). Even in this hidden and messy season, you are not overlooked. You are God's workmanship (Ephesians 2:10). You are still creative, purposeful, and beautiful, even if that creativity is now expressed differently. You are a new creation (2 Corinthians 5:17). Motherhood didn't ruin you; it's revealing the deeper you that has always been there. You are hidden in Christ (Colossians 3:3). It's okay to be unseen by the world right now because you are seen by God.

Without a clear vision for our motherhood, we may lose sight of God's desire for us to joyfully embrace our identity in Christ. As we embark on the journey of discipling our children, focusing on the bigger picture of the gospel and becoming new creations in Christ with each passing day (2 Corinthians 5:17) places a divine calling on us as mothers. In the next chapter, I will share practical ways to follow God's design as a mother and how to heed the Holy Spirit's leading.

QUESTIONS FOR REFLECTION

1. Are there ways I've stopped pursuing the intimacy with God that was cultivated during pregnancy and birth?
2. What areas of my heart or habits feel like they're drifting, and how might the Holy Spirit be inviting me to realign with Him in this new season?
3. How am I nurturing myself amidst the demands and emotions of postpartum life?
4. What specific lies, distractions, or pressures threaten to pull me out of walking by the Spirit and into striving in my own strength?
5. How can I intentionally invite God into my daily postpartum routine so motherhood becomes a place of ongoing transformation?

9

HOPE IN JESUS

WHEN THE COMFORTER COMES

Despite any hardship or trials the postpartum season might bring, the Comforter always comes. It is in these seasons of change that we have the opportunity to take God's holy invitation to become sanctified, to become more like Christ. To sanctify means to make holy, to set apart for God's purpose, to purify, and to transform into Christ's likeness. In the original Greek, the word is *"hagiazō"* (*ἁγιάζω*), meaning "to make holy, consecrate, purify, or dedicate to God."[1]

This is an ongoing process. Through my motherhood journey, God has specifically used pregnancy, childbirth, and then the forever winding road of motherhood to refine my character, remove impurities, and mold me into a version that is more like Jesus. It is in my weaknesses, the hard days full of big emotions, that this occurs.

This chapter focuses on the emotional challenges that I, along with many women, have faced (and still face) in early motherhood, including exhaustion, guilt, and comparison. The point is not to point

1. "Strong's Greek: 37. hagiazó — to make holy, consecrate," *King James Bible Online*, https://www.kingjamesbibleonline.org/strongs-number-G37/.

out the negative, but to highlight where our hope can be found and how to overcome this. The biblical hope we have for these difficult emotions isn't just about naming or focusing on the pain; it's about pointing it to Jesus and standing on Him as our firm foundation and victory. This, again, is our invitation from the Lord.

Hope does not imply that everything looks perfect; rather, it means Jesus is present, and His promises remain true. As a Christian mom, I have battled feelings of anger, struggled with comparison, and yelled when I should have prayed. I have doubted God's timing and felt inadequate. At times, I have snapped at my kids when overwhelmed, neglected to open my Bible, and pushed my husband away, trying to carry the burden alone.

Being a Christian mom doesn't mean I'm perfect. It means I acknowledge that I cannot do everything on my own and that I need a Savior. This realization has profoundly transformed my experience of motherhood and my approach to this season of life. I find hope by walking in the Spirit rather than in my flesh, and I resist the enemy's attempts to defeat me. Accepting the Lord's invitation to surrender throughout my journey to motherhood has brought me immense hope, joy, and peace.

Moreover, it has given me a purpose that transcends this temporary life. The best part of following God's design for motherhood is that we have a clear guide: the Bible. If we look to the Word of God, we can learn how to follow the Lord in this season and apply it to our daily lives. This guidance has helped me follow the Holy Spirit's leading and redirected me when necessary. The Bible is our guide and truth, but it is also alive and active (Hebrews 4:12), giving you supernatural, life-giving power. Think about that!

I want to share some biblical truth that you can speak to overcome what you might be feeling as a new mom and how to view some of these emotions through the lens of motherhood as you seek Jesus, learn your authority and identity through Him, and continue to accept His holy invitation. We must remember that emotions are very real, but how we feel is not our identity as a mother. Colossians 3:9-

10 states, *"You have stripped off your old sinful nature... Put on your new nature, and be renewed as you learn to know your Creator and become like him."* The more we behold and seek Jesus, the more we become like Him and our fruit is not manufactured by our efforts, but as a result of natural connection with Him.

ANGER

There have been many times when my toddler has thrown a tantrum while my baby cries, causing anger and frustration to rise within me. In those moments, I pause, take a deep breath, and invite the Holy Spirit into that situation to help me respond through His Spirit rather than my flesh. This doesn't always happen, and I may still react in anger at times. However, I quickly ask myself: *Am I responding out of frustration or from a place of prayer?*

Scripture tells us, *"And don't sin by letting anger control you. Don't let the sun go down while you are still angry."* (Ephesians 4:26 NLT). Jesus offers peace that calms the angry emotion inside us and teaches us to surrender our frustrations to Him. This can look like telling God that you hand over the frustrations and anger to Him and asking Him to give you patience in those moments to respond as He would.

Speaking Scripture aligns your mind with truth, allowing your responses to match your identity.

Declare: "The peace of Christ rules in my heart, guiding my responses and calming me." (Colossians 3:15)

GUILT

I have felt guilty for not being fully present with my kids, for screen time, for losing my patience, and for not doing enough. However, Jesus doesn't measure our worth by perfection. I often ask myself: *am I allowing guilt to define my identity, or am I letting grace shape my motherhood?*

As Romans 8:1 says, "*So now there is no condemnation for those who belong to Christ Jesus.*" Jesus forgives, restores, and chooses you even in your weakest moments. In moments when guilt may arise, I remember that every mistake I make is an opportunity for me to be further refined into the image of Jesus. I will never be Him, but recognizing my flaws is the first step in that direction.

Declare, "His mercies are new every morning, and I receive fresh grace for today." (Lamentations 3:22–23)

ANXIETY

As mothers, there is so much we could worry about: sleep schedules, nutrition, baby milestones, and even fears about the future. Anxiety has come to be seen as a normal part of motherhood in our society, but Jesus invites us to trade our worries for worship. When anxiety rises, I ask myself: *have I actually prayed about this before I've started to worry? Have I turned my worries into a prayer to God and asked Him for what I need?* 1 Peter 5:7 tells us to cast all our anxiety on Him because He cares for us.

Declare: "I will not be controlled by fear or worry, but I will walk in the peace of Christ that surpasses all understanding." (Philippians 4:6–7)

LONELINESS

Loneliness can be a real challenge during early motherhood. There have been times in my motherhood journey when I have gone weeks without a playdate, getting out of the house, or having any plans. Yet, I've found that Jesus is closer than the silence; you can invite Him into those quiet moments. Sometimes, I believe God allows seasons of isolation to help us grow. I ask myself: *Am I seeking connection with God in my loneliness, or am I allowing bitterness to take root?*

As Matthew 28:20 (ESV) says, "*I am with you always, to the end of the age.*" You are never truly alone; Jesus sees you, walks with you, and dwells within you. If I have learned anything about motherhood, it's that there are many seasons and they change quickly. Everything is temporary, and a lonely season can quickly end.

Declare: "Even in the quietest or hardest moments, God's Spirit surrounds me, and His presence fills every empty space." (Psalm 23:4)

DISCONTENTMENT

Discontentment can be another significant struggle as you become a mother, but I noticed a huge difference in my life before and after I found Jesus. I often longed for more rest, freedom, and, sometimes, my old life back. What Jesus did for me in this season was to shift my attitude toward gratitude.

It's a blessing to be exhausted by something I once prayed for. I continually ask myself: *Am I focusing on what I lack, or am I praising God for what I have?* As 1 Timothy 6:6 (NIV) states, "*Godliness with contentment is great gain.*" In Jesus, you have enough and are enough.

Declare: *"The Lord fills the desires of my heart according to His perfect will, and I rest in His provision."* (Psalm 37:4)

IMPATIENCE

Impatience is something I felt very strongly as a first-time mom. I wanted my baby to hit every milestone quickly, see immediate results in my postpartum fitness journey, and have another baby on my timeline. However, I finally realized that there is beauty in waiting and trusting God's timing in all things, big or small.

I often ask myself now, *What if I miss something by rushing ahead?*. Psalm 27:14 (ESV) encourages us to "*Wait for the Lord; be strong, and let your heart take courage.*" Jesus produces fruit in us, including patience, as we abide in Him. It is a fruit of His Spirit and will come naturally the more we spend time and seek Him, His ways, and His will for our lives.

Declare:"I will not grow weary in waiting, for the Lord renews my strength and directs my steps in His perfect timing." (Isaiah 40:31)

SELF-PITY

Self-pity has also crept in during difficult days when I felt no one understood what I was going through, not my mom, sister, or husband. It's so easy to fall into a "woe is me" mindset when you're in the thick of trying to navigate baby sleep, finding time for yourself, and maintaining a healthy marriage after a baby. Now, I remind myself to ask: *Am I soaking in self-pity or in God's presence and promises?*

Matthew 11:28 (NIV) tells us that Jesus's burden is light: *"Come to me, all you who are weary and burdened, and I will give you rest."* When you feel spent, Jesus sees what you sacrifice, even when it feels like no one else does. God honors unseen obedience.

Declare: "I refuse to be trapped by comparison, envy, or bitterness; instead, I rejoice in God's plan for my life." (Philippians 4:11–13)

FAILURE

Failure is something we all face. I've found myself yelling when I promised I wouldn't and feeling like I failed again. You might feel inadequate, but God's power is most evident through our surrendered weakness.

Now, when I feel like a failure, I can see how God works in those moments when the things I was trying so hard to control become a bit easier. I can see how my weaknesses, as I mother my children, are an opportunity for me to continue to be refined and sanctified. 2 Corinthians 12:9 (ESV) says, *"My grace is sufficient for you, for my power is made perfect in weakness."* Even in your failures, God is writing your redemptive story.

Declare: "I am not defined by my failures, but by the redeeming work of Jesus in my life." (Philippians 1:6)

CONTROL

Just as we try to control our circumstances and outcomes during our pregnancies and birth experience, control can creep its way in during motherhood. It's also why practicing surrender during these seasons is so important for evolving into the mom you are called to be.

When sickness spreads through the kids' church, or when my baby won't sleep despite my efforts, I've found myself trying to control every schedule, behavior, and outcome out of fear: fear of sickness and fear of a life spiraling out of control. Proverbs 3:5 (NIV) advises us to *"Trust in the Lord with all your heart and lean not on your own understanding."* So, I ask: *Am I controlling out of fear, or am I parenting from a place of trust and surrender?*

Declare: "I walk by faith, not by sight, and I trust that God is in control even when I cannot see the full picture." (2 Corinthians 5:7)

REST

You were never meant to bear the weight of motherhood alone. Physical and mental exhaustion can be a part of this journey (it starts early during pregnancy, again, as a way to prepare us for what is to come), but the exhaustion can also be an invitation to lean on Him.

What I've found is that rest isn't easy, even though I know I need it. But why is it so hard to rest? We live in a culture where rest is often equated with laziness. The busier you are, the more successful you seem. I was always the one trying to fill our weekends with plans, ensuring we had something to do. However, naps, slow days, and learning to say no can sometimes be the most spiritual things we can do.

Jesus modeled the importance of rest. Isaiah 40:29 (NLT) states, *"He gives power to the weak and strength to the powerless."* He understands your weariness and exhaustion, and He promises you supernatural strength. Ask yourself: *Am I striving in my own strength, or am I receiving supernatural rest in Christ to rejuvenate myself and be the best mom I can be?*

Declare: "My soul finds its rest in God alone. He is my refuge, my peace, and my steady place." (Psalm 62:1)

LAZINESS

My sense of laziness in motherhood stemmed from genuine apathy toward day-to-day tasks. It's easy to lose interest in the mundane and forget the significance of what we do as mothers. I often found myself asking, *why does this even matter?* But I discovered that renewing my mind with the reasons why my work as a mother matters to God is crucial.

Colossians 3:23 (NLT) says, "*Work willingly at whatever you do, as though you were working for the Lord rather than for people.*" When you work unto the Lord, even tasks like diaper changes, laundry, and dishes become a divine assignment and give you purpose.

Declare: "I am not led by apathy or procrastination—God's Spirit energizes me from within." (Philippians 2:13)

OVERWHELM

Feeling overwhelmed in my motherhood journey has always resulted from the unrealistic expectations I place on myself. I often think, *I have to get this done. I have to get that done.* But for what purpose? Does completing all the laundry make me a better mother? It doesn't.

This is where the reminder of my identity in Christ, rather than my performance, becomes vital. When to-do lists overshadow your strength, run to Jesus rather than seeking validation through performance. Psalm 61:2 (NLT) says, "*From the ends of the earth, I cry to you for help when my heart is overwhelmed. Lead me to the towering rock of safety.*" Your Savior has been there before and will carry you through difficult times.

Declare, "God has already given me what I need for this moment, this assignment, and this season." (2 Peter 1:3)

MOTHERHOOD: THE MIRROR GOD USES FOR SANCTIFICATION

I have experienced every one of these things and still do from time to time. I am sure as I enter different stages of motherhood, I will experience these differently, but being in a season with littles, impatience and anger strike me the most. I actually never considered myself a patient person before having children, and having toddlers has really tested that. The beauty of becoming a mother is that God will use these things to highlight areas that need refining.

I often wonder why God "designed" toddlers the way they are. Although some behaviors, like children's rebellious nature, are a result of the fall, it still feels as if God intentionally created His children this way, teaching us patience in motherhood right from the start. We can't always control their behavior; it's a misconception that we can control our kids. This applies whether they are infants, toddlers, teenagers, or adults.

This has been really challenging for me, but I am thankful God is teaching me how to be slow to anger and more patient now. These skills will be necessary when my children become older and face situations far beyond my control. I must trust that God's hand is over them, but also pray that they are filled with the Holy Spirit, speak and declare the word over their lives, and pray that they also learn to hear the Lord starting at a very young age. The surrender starts now.

What God invites us to experience on our journey to motherhood is a process of sanctification, refinement, and blessing. Without Jesus, motherhood can feel like drowning in demands, with worldly values fueling self-effort and personal identity rooted in achievements. It can lead us to see our children as inconveniences, avoid hardships through escapism or bitterness, and place our hope in control over circumstances or emotions. This perspective prioritizes comfort and image over the call to become more like Jesus.

PUTTING FAITH INTO PRACTICE IN MOTHERHOOD

Just as Jesus gives us hope and shifts our perspective, the Holy Spirit empowers us to navigate motherhood. After my encounter with Jesus and the subsequent freedom through Him that I received, I began to learn about what it meant to walk with Jesus, to be His true disciple and follower. I would hear Christian "lingo" and sought to understand its meaning.

During the season I was in as a new mother, God began to speak to me about how to apply these things to my postpartum experience and to motherhood as a whole. The Lord started to show me that when we learn what these truths really mean and how to live them out, we experience the fruit of the Spirit in our homes, peace when chaos rises, gentleness when tempers flare, and joy even in exhaustion.

There are many things that I have not figured out perfectly and never will, as it will be a constant process of sanctification and accepting God's invitation to continue to surrender to Him, but in this next section, I want to share how you can practically and biblically follow Jesus as a mother and how motherhood can become an opportunity to reflect Jesus's heart to our children.

DENY YOUR FLESH

"For if you live by its dictates, you will die. But if through the power of the Spirit you put to death the deeds of your sinful nature, you will live." (Romans 8:13 NIV).

Because of the fall, we are sinful by nature, inclined to respond from the flesh rather than from the Spirit of God. Denying your flesh means resisting sinful desires and choosing obedience to God instead. This includes controlling your words, reactions, and desires for comfort, food, or money.

Practical applications in motherhood may involve responding with patience instead of yelling when your child throws a tantrum, prioritizing your child's needs over your own comfort, listening to the Bible while nursing instead of scrolling, worshiping while doing dishes, or praying while rocking your baby to sleep rather than watching secular shows. This can even look like, instead of emotionally eating after a long day, praying first and choosing nourishing foods that follow God's design to support and nourish our bodies.

BEAR YOUR CROSS

"Then Jesus said to his disciples, 'If any of you wants to be my follower, you must give up your own way, take up your cross, and follow me.'" (Matthew 16:24 NLT).

Jesus endured the ultimate pain on the cross, both physically and mentally. To bear our own cross as mothers means fully surrendering to God, enduring trials with faith, and dying to self so that Christ's will can shape our lives. It's not just about enduring hardships but embracing God's purpose over our personal comfort.

The world may preach that sacrifice is a sign of weakness and that fulfillment comes from self-indulgence, but as a mother, it means trusting that sleepless nights and challenging seasons have a greater purpose and that motherhood struggles are opportunities to grow in faith. When others say you need more "me time," but God is calling you to invest in your children, you choose obedience over comfort. Rather than feeling resentful when your plans are interrupted, you pray, "Lord, help me serve my family with joy, just as you served others."

TO BE IN THE WORLD, NOT OF THE WORLD

"I have given them your word. The world hates them because they do not belong to the world, just as I do not belong to the world. I am not asking you to take them out of the world, but to keep them safe from the evil one. They do not belong to the world, just as I do not belong to the world. Make them holy by your truth; teach them your word, which is truth." (John 17:14–17 NLT).

We are called to be set apart as Christians while actively engaging with the world around us. We should be present in our community but avoid adopting its values, priorities, or ways of thinking. Instead, we must anchor ourselves in truth, not cultural trends. This might involve teaching your children biblical truths (even when it's unpopular), setting family values that reflect God's Word rather than society's standards, and carefully selecting TV shows, books, and social media content that align with biblical values and do not open doors spiritually to darkness in your home (this could be a whole separate book in itself).

Instead of overloading your family's schedule with worldly commitments or activities (birthday parties, practice, sports games, etc.), prioritize time for family devotion, church, and serving others in your community. This doesn't mean isolating your children from the world or being legalistic. As followers of Jesus, we choose to do these things because we love Jesus and trust His ways. Rather, it means prioritizing activities that help the whole family maintain a heart posture oriented toward Jesus and avoiding placing idols before Him.

RENEW YOUR MIND

"Don't copy the behavior and customs of this world, but let God transform you into a new person by changing the way you think. Then you will learn to know God's will for you, which is good and pleasing and perfect." (Romans 12:2 NLT).

Culture often encourages mothers to follow their emotions, but

God calls us to follow His Word rather than our feelings. Renewing your mind means transforming your thinking to align with God's truth instead of the world's lies.

This transformation happens by filling your heart and mind with God's Word, rejecting negative and worldly thinking, and choosing to believe and act in accordance with His truth, not based on your circumstances. Speak life and the Word over yourself and your children, rather than dwelling on struggles. Reject mom guilt and replace it with the truth of God's grace. Choose joy and gratitude in the mundane moments of motherhood. While social media, the news, and comparison can drain your joy, renewing your mind involves filling it with life-giving truth.

GUARD YOUR HEART

"Guard your heart above all else, for it determines the course of your life." (Proverbs 4:23 NLT).

In Christ, we are given a new heart (Ezekiel 36:26) and the Holy Spirit to help us discern truth from lies. We don't need to parent or make decisions based on fleeting emotions; we can walk in peace, guided by the Word of God. The world tells us to follow our hearts, but as Jeremiah 17:9 also reminds us our hearts can be extremely deceptive. Therefore, we must protect our thoughts, emotions, and spiritual well-being from things that can lead us away from God.

This is particularly crucial as a mother, as your heart directly influences how you parent, love, and lead your family. This might look like choosing faith-filled content instead of shows that promote unhealthy relationships or fear-based narratives. Instead of comparing yourself to other moms, practice gratitude and contentment. Rather than saying yes to every playdate or responsibility, carve out time for prayer, worship, and quiet reflection to replenish your spirit.

DO EVERYTHING AS UNTO THE LORD

"Work willingly at whatever you do, as though you were working for the Lord rather than for people." (Colossians 3:2 NLT).

In the eyes of the world, motherhood is often reduced to productivity, appearances, and self-fulfillment rather than faithfulness. Doing everything "as unto the Lord" means that every task, no matter how big or small, should be performed with excellence and love, seeking to glorify God. When you fold laundry, change diapers, or prepare meals, offer these acts as acts of love to God.

Correcting and training children can be exhausting, but when approached with the mindset of shaping their hearts for Christ, it becomes a form of ministry. Rather than nagging or criticizing, choose to encourage and pray for your husband, remembering that your marriage is a testimony of God's love.

WALK BY THE SPIRIT

"So I say, let the Holy Spirit guide your lives. Then you won't be doing what your sinful nature craves." (Galatians 5:16 NLT).

I've mentioned this concept many times: it's about daily dependence on the Holy Spirit, allowing Him to guide your thoughts, actions, and decisions rather than following the desires of your flesh. This necessitates ongoing surrender to God, prioritizing His ways over your own.

The world often justifies anger, frustration, or selfishness as "just part of motherhood," and no, you're not expected to be perfect, but Jesus didn't leave you to figure motherhood out on your own. He sent His Spirit to dwell in you, help you, and produce fruit through you.

Practical ways to apply this in motherhood include inviting the Holy Spirit to lead you before your day begins, praying before making parenting decisions instead of acting on impulse, creating a peaceful atmosphere by welcoming the Holy Spirit into your home, and asking God for patience and discernment when your children challenge you. When your child is upset, instead of simply fixing the problem, take the time to pray with them.

Without the Word of God, walking by the Spirit would be nearly impossible. Hebrews 4:12 NLT says, *"For the word of God is alive and powerful. It is sharper than the sharpest two-edged sword, cutting between soul and spirit, between joint and marrow. It exposes our innermost thoughts and desires."* It is the Word of God that truly transforms us as mothers, and the more we hear it (Romans 10:17), the more we have faith in it, and the more we obey it and walk in it.

LEARNING GRACE THROUGH DAILY PRACTICE

God uses every season of our lives to teach, refine, sanctify, and guide us if we allow Him. It's a partnership that definitely requires effort.

He gently guides us like a shepherd and never condemns us for not getting it right. You will not be perfect. You might forget to pray before raising your voice. There will be times when you act out of your flesh instead of the Spirit. However, the more you invite God into your everyday moments, the more peace you will experience and the more joy you will discover.

You may wonder how to spend quality time with Jesus as a busy mom. There will be times when you feel disconnected from God, but that doesn't mean He is far away. You might not have quiet time, and sometimes, worship may look like nursing in the dark while whispering Jesus' name. That, too, is worship, and He remains close.

As mothers, we can be very hard on ourselves. We often have expectations of how we want our days to go, but with kids, those expectations can easily be thrown out the window. There have been days when I woke up early to spend quiet time with Jesus, only to have all of my kids wake up early, too. Or I may have a master plan to read and worship while my kids nap, only to find that their nap schedules completely clash.

It can be frustrating to want that alone time with God, to follow Jesus, to be the mom He's called you to be, and to feel like you're trying so hard to make it work, but it doesn't happen. The important thing to remember is that Jesus wants a relationship with us and is more than happy to be a part of our daily lives. He invites us to be partners with Him in everything: cooking, cleaning, managing tantrums, and dealing with sibling fights.

Jesus is always near. We can talk to Him and spend time with Him at any time. While having a secret place for quiet time is important, it's essential to give yourself grace in this season.

The Lord says, *"My grace is all you need. My power works best in weakness."* (2 Corinthians 12:9 NLT). He isn't measuring the length of your devotional time or disappointed if your worship was interrupted by a hungry toddler. He doesn't care about how many scriptures you read in a day. Instead, He sees the longing in your heart and meets you amidst the chaos, the interruptions, the mess, the noise, and the neediness. Motherhood is not an obstacle to intimacy with Jesus; rather, it is the very place where He invites you into deeper surrender, greater trust, and abundant grace.

You might picture your walk with God looking a certain way, perhaps with a quiet house, a cup of coffee in hand, a Bible open before you, and long hours of worship and journaling. But in this season, God may be asking, *"Will you still invite me in when the quiet is gone? Will you meet me in the noise? Will you surrender your expectations of how it should look?"* Surrender isn't just about laying down your plans once; it's a daily choice to lay them down again. This, again, is God's holy invitation.

God's invitation isn't about checking off spiritual boxes; it's about becoming more like Jesus as we rely on Him during the hardest days of motherhood. Surrender isn't weakness; it's worship. In surrender, we discover strength not of our own but through Jesus.

QUESTIONS FOR REFLECTION

1. Where do your expectations for quiet time with God conflict with real life?
2. What interrupted you this week, and how might that have been an invitation from God?
3. Which emotions, anger, guilt, or overwhelm, are shaping your responses right now? Are you willing to surrender those feelings?
4. How could you turn one daily task into a moment with Jesus?
5. What is one area where you need to trade control for trust?

10

A HIGH CALLING

MOTHERHOOD AS A MINISTRY

What is the goal of motherhood? What are your hopes and dreams for your children?

Before I met Jesus, I allowed the world's standards and cultural norms to define these questions. I sought answers from the world rather than from God. However, the world's advice on parenting and what it means to be a "good" parent often differs significantly from what God teaches.

As mothers, we are constantly surrounded by voices telling us what we should be, do, or believe. There is a vast array of conflicting advice on how to parent. Should you breastfeed or bottle-feed? Co-sleep or sleep train? Send your child to public school or homeschool? The internet, social media, and even well-meaning friends often shape our picture of what "good motherhood" looks like. Many of these messages sound positive on the surface, yet when we look more deeply, we realize they often lead to exhaustion, striving, or comparison rather than peace and purpose.

I don't share this to point fingers or create guilt, but because I've lived through many of these cultural pressures myself. At one time or another, I've worn the badge of the "busy martyr mom," compared my home to others online, or sought identity in productivity and perfection.

My goal in naming these mindsets isn't to condemn but to bring awareness, to help us pause and ask, "Is this belief rooted in God's truth or the world's pressure?" When we can recognize where culture has shaped our motherhood, we can surrender those mindsets to the Lord and allow Him to redefine what motherhood looks like through His Word and Spirit.

These cultural messages often conflict with the call to a holy, spirit-led, and purposeful motherhood (I have been there). I want to look at a few of these common "mom cultures" or mindsets that I, along with many other mothers, have encountered and explore how they contrast with God's design for motherhood.

MOMMY MARTYR

This mindset promotes the idea that mothers must do everything alone, sacrificing their well-being for their families. It glamorizes burnout, self-pity, and resentment, where exhaustion is worn like a badge of honor, often accompanied by the feeling that no one sees or helps.

HOT-MESS MOM

This mindset embraces lateness, disorganization, and chaos, often making dysfunction seem humorous and relatable. There's little effort to grow, organize, or take ownership because, after all, we're all "hot messes," right?

PINTEREST-PERFECT MOM

Here, your worth is linked to aesthetics and creativity. There is immense pressure to host perfect parties, dress children in color-coordinated outfits, and maintain a magazine-ready home, often at the expense of your peace and sanity.

SELF-CARE-OBSESSED MOM

This ideology holds that "you can't pour from an empty cup," advocating self-prioritization. While rest is essential, this culture can sometimes justify neglecting one's calling or family in the name of self-care.

BOSS MOM

This mindset suggests that if you're not making money or building a brand, you're wasting time. It glorifies productivity and wealth, often making stay-at-home mothering or slower seasons of life feel inadequate.

COMPARISON-COMPETITIVE MOM

Here, other mothers set the standard for success. Fueled by social media, this culture turns motherhood into a competition: Whose child walks first? Whose house is cleaner? Who bounced back faster after pregnancy?

HANDS-OFF, CHILD-INDEPENDENCE MINDSET

This permissive approach suggests that mothers should neither train nor discipline their children, allowing them to explore freely without guidance. It promotes the idea that boundaries are harsh.

MOM-GUILT MINDSET

This pervasive mindset instills the belief that mothers are never doing enough and are always failing. This mindset often keeps mothers trapped in a cycle of constant shame. No matter what they do, they feel like they're messing everything up. It promotes a culture of numbing and escapism. We moms escape with our phones, binge-watch shows, indulge in snacks, scroll through social media, or maybe even turn to substances. This quiet epidemic steals peace and presence from the home and dulls a mother's spiritual awareness.

CHILD-AS-IDOL MINDSET

This is where your child becomes everything to the point of defining your life. While this may seem admirable at first, if your identity is entirely tied to your child, you risk being crushed by their failures and burdening them with emotional weights they were never meant to carry.

Surrounded by these cultural norms, pressures, and mindsets, it's easy to lose sight of what God intended for us as mothers, leaving many to silently navigate these challenges.

I understand this all too well. After having my first baby, I encountered almost every one of these cultural pressures and felt their weight. On challenging days, instead of accepting help, I insisted on doing everything myself. I pushed away support from family and even my husband, taking on the role of a martyr.

I would often say things like, "I always forget the diaper bag" or "I'm such an unprepared mom." Getting ready to leave was always chaotic, yet I didn't realize I was agreeing to a chaotic lifestyle. If we were heading to an event or party, I also felt the need to ensure my kids were perfectly matched and that my house looked immaculate, as if no one lived there. I noticed other moms going out for "mom's night out" and felt pressured to do the same.

Maybe that's where some women find refreshment in motherhood. Perhaps that's how I thought I could fill my cup. I felt the competitive drive for my kids to hit every milestone first: crawling, walking, and talking. Seeing my children excel made me feel more worthy as a mother. One evening, my husband came home from work, and I told him I needed a glass of wine because it was the only way I could unwind after a long day with my toddler.

I share these experiences because, while I don't like that they reflect my reality, they are true. Many moms experience similar feelings, and I want you to know it's okay. We are human, and God doesn't expect perfection in motherhood; however, He does provide a supernatural power for us to be set apart and prosperous in our motherhood journey!

I've actually always felt like an outcast, but now, trying to follow Jesus in motherhood, I feel even more like I'm in the minority. I don't say this negatively, but I do know this is why Jesus says the *"path is narrow"* to follow Him (Matthew 7:13–14). I wanted to be someone who truly followed Jesus, not just believed in Him, and I encourage you to do the same.

When my husband and I started to follow Jesus, our friend circles changed completely. We naturally stopped hanging out with certain people, not because we thought they didn't follow Jesus, but because it was a part of our transformation. I see it as God's protection, guiding us to form new relationships with those who live their lives more biblically and encourage us in our faith.

We found a church shortly after we committed our lives to Christ. This experience greatly influenced our perspective, helping us realize that we didn't have to conform to cultural norms. Just as I had seen that God's design and His ways are different for pregnancy and childbirth, I began to understand that God's ways are different in motherhood and parenting. As we interacted with people living these kinds of lives, we saw their thriving, authentic peace. It was not a superficial kind of peace, but something truly different. We began to feel that same peace as well.

I understand that some people might think, *I don't want to follow all these rules; I just want to go along with the world and its culture.* However, I've learned that following the world does not bring true peace or joy like Jesus offers. Although I was never miserable before, I often faced anxiety and comparison (and many other things I've already mentioned in this book).

It wasn't until I embraced Jesus that I found true contentment and genuine joy, especially that deep-seated peace. Life following Jesus came with an easy yoke and light burden!

This is the encouragement I want to offer you. Yes, the path Jesus invites us to walk may be narrow, but it leads us to an abundant life that the world cannot offer.

Instead of the "mommy martyr" culture, Jesus invites us to serve with joy, not resentment, and to rest in Him. You are not alone. You are yoked with Christ (Matthew 11:28–30). Instead of the "hot-mess mom" culture, God brings order out of chaos. He calls us to be transformed and to create a spirit-led, peaceful home, even amidst the mess (1 Corinthians 14:33; Romans 12:2). Instead of striving for a "Pinterest-perfect mom" image, you can remember that God looks at the heart, not your highlight reel. Your child doesn't need perfection; they need a present, spirit-filled mom (1 Samuel 16:7).

Rather than fitting into a "self-care obsessed" culture, true rest is found in Christ, not just in spa days (though those can be nice, too, and are still needed). God calls us to serve Him in strength, not to idolize ourselves (Isaiah 40:31; John 15:5). Instead of the "boss babe hustle" mentality, God says your value lies in your obedience. While He may call you to build, He also honors hidden, faithful stewardship (Colossians 3:23; Luke 16:10).

Rather than succumbing to comparison, you can run your own race with your eyes fixed on Jesus. There's grace for the path God has set for you (Hebrews 12:1–2; Galatians 6:4). Instead of adopting a "hands-off, child-led independence" approach, remember that God disciplines those He loves, calling mothers to train, teach, and disciple their children in love (Proverbs 22:6; Hebrews 12:11).

Rather than giving in to "mom guilt," remember that Jesus says there is no condemnation for those in Christ. Your identity is secure, and God covers your weaknesses with grace (Romans 8:1; 2

Corinthians 12:9). Instead of engaging in numbing escapism, know that Jesus doesn't merely numb your pain; He heals it. He delivers life, offering more than just temporary fixes (John 14:13–14). Instead of idolizing children, God calls us to love our children deeply but to worship Him alone. Children are like arrows, not altars (Psalm 127:3–5).

MOTHERHOOD AS A MINISTRY

As mothers, we are created with strong maternal instincts to love, nurture, and instruct. However, in a culture that often strays from biblical principles, this can become confusing and distracting.

Being "just a mom" is not always regarded as a high calling in our society, but to God, it truly is. The Bible presents motherhood as a holy and sacred role, designed by God and deeply connected to His heart for creation, legacy, and spiritual formation. While there is no single verse that explicitly states motherhood is your calling, Scripture is rich with themes, stories, and direct commands that affirm motherhood as a divine assignment.

Motherhood is a God-given role within His creation, as seen in Genesis 1:28. Children are blessings, not burdens (Psalm 127:3), and motherhood is also a place for discipleship (Deuteronomy 6:6–7).

Moreover, motherhood reflects the nurturing nature of God (Isaiah 66:13) and serves as part of a legacy and spiritual inheritance (2 Timothy 1:5). In a world that may devalue or overlook this role, God elevates motherhood as a vital aspect of building His kingdom.

Let's look at the ministry of motherhood. First, what is biblical ministry? It is service to God and to others, motivated by love, empowered by the Holy Spirit, and carried out in obedience to God's Word. Ministry is not limited to the pulpit or church leadership; rather, it encompasses serving God's purposes in the world. The Greek term for ministry is "diakonia," which means service, particularly characterized by humility and selflessness.

Jesus said, *"But among you it will be different. Whoever wants to be a leader among you must be your servant, and whoever wants to be first among you must become your slave. For even the Son of Man came not to be served but to serve others and to give his life as a ransom for many"* (Matthew 20:26–28 NLT). Rooted in servanthood, ministry is done in the power of the Holy Spirit and anchored in love and truth, all for the glory of God rather than oneself. When we view motherhood as a ministry, we recognize the role of raising, nurturing, and discipling our children as a sacred calling from God. More than just a role, responsibility, or season of life, it's a divine assignment with eternal significance.

Just as Jesus's ministry involved daily acts of self-sacrifice, so does motherhood. You're not merely raising children; you're discipling souls, nurturing life, and reflecting the heart of the Father. Jesus's ministry provides the foundation for the ministry of motherhood. This is your invitation to follow in His footsteps.

Jesus came not to be served but to serve, just as mothers pour themselves out daily for their families, whether seen or unseen. Jesus was obedient to His Father's will (John 6:38), and similarly, godly mothers submit to God's will even when it is challenging. Jesus spoke in love and corrected gently, just as mothers teach and train with both truth and a gentle touch.

Jesus ministered to the weak, sick, and lost, just as mothers care for their children when they are physically and emotionally vulnerable. Jesus faced misunderstanding, rejection, and sacrifice, much like godly mothers who endure pain and exhaustion and often remain unseen but persist because they love their children. Jesus multiplied life spiritually, just as mothers nurture, give birth to, and multiply life both physically and spiritually.

Jesus invited people into a relationship with the Father, just as godly mothers create a home environment where children can learn about Him. Jesus was empowered by the Holy Spirit (Luke 4:1), and mothers should also rely on the Spirit for strength, guidance, comfort, and conviction.

Throughout my journey in motherhood, I've realized that ministry begins from day one. As a mother to young children, it's easy to believe that early moments don't matter, but the truth is that every moment counts. We are shaping our children into who they will become from infancy.

I felt God urging me not to wait to be released into ministry; I was already in one. Just as a missionary goes to a different country to share the gospel, a mother is called to her children. Motherhood is not a detour from real ministry; it is real ministry. You are raising souls to know and love Jesus, teaching your children to pray, seek God's voice, and trust Him. The command to go out and make disciples begins at home.

Whether it's sacrificing sleep to comfort a sick child or putting aside your desires for the needs of your family, these acts of love reflect Christ's compassion. When done unto the Lord, even the most mundane tasks become acts of worship. A mother's love is patient, forgiving, and nurturing, and it also reveals aspects of God's character. When your children experience grace, gentleness, and truth through you, they are encountering Jesus through your parenting. What an eye-opening realization this was for me.

CHOOSING THE WAY OF JESUS

Being a Christian mom means something very different from what I initially thought. Before I truly met Jesus, I viewed being a Christian as merely a religion or a label that people used to identify themselves, and I honestly believed they were somehow superior.

When someone proclaimed, "I'm a Christian," it sounded like they were saying, "I'm better than you," or "I have my life all figured out." But that is actually the opposite of what being a Christian means, especially as a mother. To be a Christian is to be a follower of Christ. Following Him means letting go of the world's ways, embracing the ways of Jesus, and accepting His holy invitation.

You must surrender everything and rewire your thinking. What I have learned is that following Jesus might require some lifestyle changes, but as soon as I began to surrender my life to Him, I somehow found that my life became easier.

I found that partnering with God's Word instead of the world to guide me on this journey, my life got better. On days when I felt like *God, I don't know how I am going to do this,* and I replaced it with *God, thank you that you are chasing me down with goodness and mercy all the days of my life* (Psalm 23:6), things started to flow. When I remembered that I can only surrender something that God has given me in the first place, I felt peace. When I started taking all parts of the Bible seriously, not just what was convenient for my lifestyle, blessings started to follow suit (Deuteronomy 28).

It's interesting because, in practical terms, my life became much more challenging after finding Jesus: more kids, more responsibilities, a new business, and new stresses. Yet, the burdens of life began to feel so much lighter.

So, why am I sharing this?

Because I wish someone had told me that motherhood doesn't begin when your baby is in your arms. It begins with a holy invitation at the moment you discover you're pregnant. From the kicks in your belly to the night waking with a newborn, Jesus invites you to walk with Him, not just during the big moments but in every single one.

Becoming a mother is not just a physical journey; it is a deeply spiritual one. The very moment you conceive, God is not only forming a baby in your womb but also shaping you into the mother your child needs, one who is led by the Spirit, not the world.

That positive pregnancy test was never simply biological; it was part of your calling. It was an invitation to surrender and partner with God in bringing forth life and raising that life to know Him.

Many days, I fall short of following Jesus. I will never be perfect, as only He is, but I will continue to focus on Him to guide my path. Although we will never be perfect, we can continue to align our thoughts, words, and actions with the truth and speak highly of ourselves as mothers and this calling.

You are a great mom, or maybe you're not one yet. I know you will be when the time comes. You don't have to have it all figured out. Jesus is waiting for you to seek Him every day and to say yes.

Yes to His ways, yes to His design, yes to His blueprint, and yes to His help. Yes to His Spirit, yes to His holy invitation. It all starts with a simple yes.

"He tends His flocks like a shepherd; He gathers the lambs in His arms and carries them close to His heart. He gently leads those that have young" (Isaiah 40:11 NLT).

REFLECTION QUESTIONS

1. When you think about motherhood as a spiritual journey rather than just a physical one, what changes in the way you view your daily life as a mom (or future mom)?
2. How has God been shaping your heart, character, or faith through motherhood (or the desire for motherhood)?
3. In what ways have you felt the world's influence more than the Holy Spirit's guidance in how you mother (or prepare to mother)?
4. What does surrender look like for you in this season of motherhood? What might God be asking you to release control over?
5. How can you practically say yes to God's design for motherhood today?
6. Which part of Isaiah 40:11 speaks most to you right now? (*"He gathers the lambs... He gently leads those that have young."*) What does that reveal about God's heart toward you as a mother?
7. How can you remind yourself that you don't have to be

perfect, that Jesus is your source of grace and guidance in motherhood?

8. What lies or pressures from culture have you believed about motherhood that you want to replace with God's truth?
9. How does knowing that God is forming both you and your child give you peace or perspective about your journey?

CONCLUSION

You've reached the final pages of *A Labor of Grace*, but this is not the end. Instead, it's the beginning of a holy, Spirit-led journey. This book was never meant to be just words on paper. I didn't write it because I have all the answers, but I do have a message. This was a call, an invitation, to walk through pregnancy, birth, and motherhood with God, not in your own strength, not according to the fear-driven narratives of the world, but anchored in truth, carried by grace, and led by the Holy Spirit.

We've torn down some of the cultural lies that God has made visible to me. We've exposed the idols of control, fear, and self-reliance throughout this journey to motherhood. We've changed our perspective to see this season and journey not as a burden, but as a refining, sanctifying, and sacred process.

You were never meant to journey alone. You were meant to walk in step with the Helper, the Comforter, the Advocate, the Spirit of Truth. I pray these pages have helped you see pregnancy, childbirth, and motherhood as a holy assignment from God, helped you trade fear for faith and control for trust, helped you hear God's voice more clearly in this season, and helped you step into motherhood not with anxiety, but with boldness and peace.

Seeing God's holy invitation is about living under the full gospel of the Kingdom, saying yes to God's Kingdom plans instead of just "being saved and surviving." You were made for such a time as this.

Thank you for letting me speak into your story. It's an honor that I do not take lightly. And now? I'm cheering you on as you step into what's next. You don't have to be perfect. You just have to surrender. From that posture, everything changes. Your womb becomes a place of worship. Your motherhood becomes your ministry. Your daily moments become Kingdom work.

If this book stirred something in you, if you're ready to walk this journey even deeper, I'd love to invite you into my online space by scanning the QR code on the following page. I regularly share encouragement, teaching, and practical tools to help women like you prepare for birth and motherhood God's way.

THANK YOU FOR READING MY BOOK!

Just to say thank you for buying my book, I would like to connect!
Scan the QR Code Here:

I appreciate your interest in my book and value your feedback, as it helps me improve future versions. I would appreciate it if you could leave your invaluable review on Amazon.com with your feedback. Thank you!

www.ingramcontent.com/pod-product-compliance
Lightning Source LLC
LaVergne TN
LVHW090525110826
845146LV00003B/983

9798901584002